Comedian at Law

From Courtrooms to Comedy, Anxiety, and Clients Who Wanted Me Dead

Nick Leydorf

Comedian at Law: From Courtrooms to Comedy, Anxiety, and Clients Who Wanted Me Dead

© 2025 Nick Leydorf

For permissions, contact:
Leydorf Law Firm, PLLC
321 W. Lake Lansing Rd.
East Lansing, MI 48823

ISBN: 979-8-9999908-0-8

Printed in the United States of America

To my wife and son—
the only jury whose verdict really matters.

Chapter List

Disclaimer
(a/k/a "Please Don't Disbar Me")

This book is about my life as a lawyer. Yes, lawyers actually *do* have lives. But here's the deal:

- **No client secrets were harmed in the making of this book.** Names, dates, places, and details have been changed, shuffled, and occasionally tossed into a blender to make sure nobody can be identified. If you think you recognize yourself in these pages, you're wrong. You're flattering yourself. Stop it.

- **Attorney–client privilege and confidentiality are still a thing.** I'm not spilling anyone's beans. (Except maybe my own, and they were overcooked long ago.)

- **Any resemblance to actual persons, living or dead, is purely coincidental.** Unless I'm talking about myself. Then it's tragically accurate.

- **No legal advice is given here.** If you use this book as a guide to handle your legal problems, that's on you. That's like using a cookbook to perform surgery. Please don't.

For those who need authority (I see you, fellow attorneys), this disclaimer is supported by *See Generally, Common Sense v. Oversharing*, 404 U.S. LOL (2012) and *Restatement (Second) of Things I'd Like to Keep My Bar License*, § 1.01(a).

In short: this is my story, not a case file. It's about how practicing law shaped me, occasionally broke me, and sometimes made me laugh when laughing seemed impossible. The rest is fiction, or at least legally unprovable.

My Client Threatened to Kill Me

"I'm gonna kill you and all y'all motherfuckers on this motherfucking case." Hearing those words confirmed what I already knew - becoming a lawyer had been a terrible mistake. The man, my soon-to-be-former client, said those words in an eerily calm way, like this wasn't the first time he'd threatened someone's life.

For years, I kicked around the idea that maybe I had picked the wrong career. Maybe I hitched my wagon to the wrong horse, or star, or whatever that saying is. However, after those words poured out of his mouth, there wasn't time for second-guessing my career choice. Even though there was a fence-like, steel divider between us, my brain didn't care. It was a weird room to begin with. Instead of plexiglass, they put a chain link fence on top of a large steel table to keep people apart. There was no way he could hurt me, unless he had a blow dart smuggled up his ass.

I felt a wave of panic wash over me. It was like someone put a blanket of a thousand tiny needles over my back and arms. My brain did whatever my brain does, analyzed the situation, and came up with "Hey, you're locked in an attorney-client visitation room in the Eaton County Jail in Charlotte, Michigan, with a dude that just threatened your life; you need to get the fuck out of here."

But under the panic of something heavier – shame. Shame that I spent twelve years in this profession and somehow ended up here, locked in a room with a man who hated me enough to want me dead. I wondered if he was just saying what I had been too scared to admit: that I had made the wrong choice in becoming a lawyer. That this career wasn't just draining me – it was actively destroying me. Have I wasted my life? I told myself there's no way to change careers now. You're stuck, bud.

But I wanted out. Not from just the room, but from the person I had become in the suit helplessly sitting there. I wasn't fearless. I wasn't noble. I wasn't Atticus Finch. I was just a scared kid from Bannister, Michigan, who happened to memorize enough law to trick people into thinking I had my shit together.

Childhood

My formative years were spent in the desolate and mundane town of Bannister, Michigan - a place that drains all color and excitement from your soul. A place where time moves as slowly and stagnantly as the murky field run off that forms the southern boundary where I grew up on Woodbridge Road. A place so devoid of stimulation, you can feel your brain cells wither away with each passing day.

I don't feel bad saying that. If someone from Bannister is reading this book right now, I'm sure they're like, "Yeah, Nick's description was apt." Bannister is a "town" (not sure what classifies as a town, or village, or place where dreams die) of less than 100 people 45 minutes north, northeast of Lansing, Michigan's capital. Yes, I said "north, northeast" because I've never used that way to describe a direction, so I wanted to give it a whirl.

While it isn't much to look at now, Bannister has the carcass of a place that used to be something. It looked like it used to have a grain elevator next to the train tracks. "Used to" is the phrase that I associate with Bannister the most. It used to have a grain elevator. It used to have two bars right next to each other, until someone figured out that you could get the same shitty beer in both bars, and the other one became obsolete. Someone told me that there were two bars, so if you got kicked out of one, you could go right next door and continue to get plastered. It has train tracks that slice through it, but they don't have any gates that keep you from crossing the tracks when a train is coming. Which tells you that even Bannister doesn't give a shit about people who live in Bannister. They're like "Hey, if you're stupid enough to live here, you're on your own."

I don't think I'm going out on a limb by saying that I'm the most famous person from Bannister. It's not that I have a puffed-up view of myself; it's more like no one from Bannister has ever achieved anything more than teenage pregnancy or being able to burp the alphabet, so someone who managed to become a lawyer is a pretty big fucking deal. I'm still waiting for the parade in my honor.

I grew up on Woodbridge Road, which is about a mile east of the greater Bannister downtown metropolitan area. The road is not paved. It's made of dirt or ground-up bones from the people who never made it out. I asked for confirmation from the township clerk, but as of printing, they have never confirmed or denied my suspicions about the road composition. So I lived a quarter mile north on this dirt road, possibly made of human bone.

For the first 13 years of my life, and I don't mean to brag, I lived in a trailer. Even though I lived in one for over a decade, I'm not sure if it's a trailer or a mobile home. I'm not sure about the vernacular. It didn't have wheels, which I guess is worse because we were stuck there on Woodbridge Road. It wasn't even a double-wide; it was a single-wide trailer that was about 3 feet away from my great-grandfather's house. It wasn't much. It had a kitchen, a living room, two bedrooms, and a bathroom half the size of a normal human being. It also had a smoke alarm that went off incessantly. It wouldn't even need smoke for it to go off. It'd be a regular smokeless Saturday afternoon, and that fucking thing would go off. It wouldn't have been so annoying if it weren't so

4

goddamn loud. I honestly think that thing was responsible for a lot of my anxiety. Maybe I could represent myself in my own class action lawsuit? Each time the alarm blared, my heart would race and my body would tense up in fear. It wasn't just noise—it was proof that I wasn't safe anywhere, not even in my own home. I'd sit frozen, waiting for someone to notice how much it scared me, waiting for a hug or a laugh to cut the tension. But no one ever said anything. The fear just echoed inside me until it became a permanent background hum, the static channel of my childhood. Looking back, it's not surprising that later in life the buzz of a jailhouse door would send me straight back here, to a kid who never learned how to feel safe. The sudden jolt of sound felt like a slap to the face, jarring me from my thoughts and sending adrenaline coursing through my veins. I never could get used to its shrill, piercing tone, always catching me off guard, no matter how many times it went off before. It was a constant source of anxiety, an unwelcome interruption in my otherwise quiet existence.

This alarm made me feel alone and emotionally isolated. I longed for comfort, but I was afraid to ask for help. Fast forward 30+ years later, when I became what some would describe as a "successful" adult, but I still longed for comfort and was afraid to ask for help for fear of being rejected.

Dollars to donuts, I'm sure that it would go off when my mom was pregnant with me, too. It was as emotionally jarring as it was loud. That sound that I can't describe in words here will forever be inside my brain. I know that a lot of people have struggled with more in their childhood, but hey, this thing was pretty fucking loud and scared the shit out of me every time. It's not like this thing was going to prevent a fire anyway, and the closest fire department was like 25 minutes away. This trailer was going to burn quicker than Snoop Dogg's blunt. I don't know why we didn't just disconnect the thing and take our chances. Who knows, maybe I could have become president if I hadn't had to suffer through that thing?

I should probably talk about my parents and not just a smoke alarm. My parents are Jeff and Kathy Leydorf. My dad also had a last name, so his name was Jeff Leydorf, not just Jeff. That would have been more interesting if my dad just had one name like Prince, but then he would have probably been the most famous Bannistarian. They are genuinely nice people. No one put out lit cigarettes on my arm or smushed my face in potato salad or anything like that.

I don't have any brothers or sisters, so if you're good at deductive reasoning, by now you've figured out that I'm an only child. "Only child" sounds like "lonely child," which is pretty depressing. It was pretty lonely being an only kid growing up in the middle of nowhere. Our nearest neighbor was like a mile away, and there was a kid who lived there who was my age, but he smelled bad so I didn't play with him a lot, only when my loneliness was greater than the smell did we really hang out. I'm sure he doesn't smell bad now so sorry, my dude, for putting your cleanliness on blast.

Most of the time, it was just me and my thoughts. I don't remember us talking about our feelings or anything like that, because if we did, I would have definitely brought up that fucking smoke alarm - "Hey, we need to get rid of that goddamn thing!" I have no recollection of ever discussing our emotions as a family. While my parents were always kind, I can't help but imagine how comforting it would have been to sit down and openly share our feelings. Instead, much of my childhood was spent in dullness and isolation, with only my own thoughts for company.

Throughout my childhood, my parents had steady jobs. My mom was a graphic designer and worked in Lansing, which was about 45 minutes away from our "house" in Bannister. Monday through Friday, she would get up real stupid early in the morning and drive to Lansing. She'd do whatever graphic designer moms do and then leave work about 4:30 pm and be home about 5:15 pm.

I don't remember seeing her a lot during the week. She was a very hard worker. There were times when she would remember that she didn't do something right and would go to the office on the weekend to fix it. She was very dedicated to her job, sometimes to the point that it was excessive. I observed the behavior and noted that it seemed to be the accepted method of operation. Despite not being in a work setting, tasks and responsibilities would often spill over into personal time without hesitation or concern.

Even as I'm writing this, I'm judging myself. To the Bannister Bar patron, part of me, I sound like a toddler. "It made me sad when my mommy would work a lot." If the more enlightened part of me were to retort, I'd say, "If you sound like a toddler, it's because your family never discussed emotions." I remember my dad saying, "Kath, don't worry about it." There wasn't a discussion about what she was worried about and why she was worrying. What would happen if she just finished it on Monday? All I know is that she did worry about it. I felt that. It was like static inside of me. If you're an old head like me, before there was cable and streaming, anything you wanted at any time, there was just a dial on the television. If there were no channel, there would just be static on the television. That's what it felt like to me as a kid. Uncomfortable and loud. I didn't grow up with anyone else, so I didn't know if that was normal or not. I still don't know, because it's not like I can just start over again. Now that I'm older, I wish we had talked more because there are things that I think would have been helpful to discuss about choosing the right career, and partner, and how rewarding yourself with food all the time may mean you never want to take your shirt off in public.

My dad was an art teacher at Ovid-Elsie High School. He got that job right after college and worked there until he retired. He wasn't physically affectionate with me. He would jokingly tell me, "Get away from me," when I'd try to hug him. Even in our playful moments, there was a distance between us that I couldn't ignore. I'm not sure why he was like that, because he didn't talk about his relationship with his parents. I'm guessing his mom and dad weren't physically affectionate with him either. It turns out that getting hugs and things like that is pretty important to me and something that I wish I had been able to experience. I didn't know that it was okay to tell your parents that because we didn't talk about our feelings. I was a child going through these emotions on my own. I was never taught how to talk about my feelings, so I felt lost and alone in these emotions.

Here's the Bannister closed-off part of me again. I don't want this to come off as me bitching about how I grew up. Come on, I was a white kid growing up in the '80s. I didn't suffer much. We never got evicted. There was always food in the house. No one molested me. But there were things about it that I didn't like. It's taken me a long time to be able to say that it's okay that I felt that way. Being a white kid doesn't mean that there weren't parts of my childhood that I didn't enjoy.

Growing up, discipline in my household meant physical punishment. It wasn't uncommon for me to receive a belt on my ass as a form of correction. But as I grew older, I began to realize how wrong and hurtful this method was. On one hand, I understood that it was meant to teach me right from wrong. But on the other hand, it left me feeling completely worthless and questioning if I deserved such treatment. The inner conflict between understanding the intention behind the punishment and hating the way it made me feel constantly plagued me. It made me feel like I was less than a human being. It made me fear my parents. I felt betrayed by them and alone when I'd have to sit in my room alone after being hit with that belt. All those years ago, getting the belt only instilled fear inside me. Fear of authority figures and the fear of what would happen if I lost control.

Hitting someone with a belt - that's the kind of shit people did in the 1800s when your horse or donkey didn't do what you wanted it to. You don't treat a human being like that. However, for my parents and grandparents, it didn't seem like a big deal. Spare the rod and spoil the child was the phrase I heard. Fuck whoever came up with that.

I want to be clear. I forgive them for what they did. They're not bad people. I realize that my parents thought that was okay because they experienced it from their own families. It doesn't make it right, but it's not like my parents one day got up and decided that if their kid did something that they didn't like, they were going to hit him with a belt. However, I don't excuse what they did either.

The time after being hit with a belt was horrible because it meant that I would spend time in my room crying alone. Even more alone than I was before I did the thing that angered them. I couldn't take that. When your family has only three people in it that don't talk all that much, you really don't like being left alone in your room with an ass that stings from being hit with a belt.

My dad didn't seem that interested in being a dad. He was always physically present, but I felt like I was a bother. He was passionate about studying our family history. That started when I was in middle school. He would connect with other people named Leydorf around the United States and in Europe to try and piece together our family's history. He'd spend hours at home into all hours of the night doing that. He was a teacher and would have summers off, and that is what he would do in the summers. We wouldn't take trips together, he'd stay in his room and study dead people. It made me feel like I wasn't valuable enough to him. I was a Leydorf that was alive in the next room, but he'd rather invest his time in the dead Leydorfs. Some of them lived in Germany in the 1940s, so you know they did some fucked up shit. I'm sure there was a Leydorf that was Hitler's pool man or tennis coach, so why the fuck are you spending so much time doing it?

We did take one trip that I remember to Ohio. You know what they say about Ohio, it's the Paris of the Midwest. We didn't go to Ohio to go to Cedar Point, but to talk to some old lady about her dead relatives. Then the cherry on top was swinging by a cemetery to take pictures of tombstones. I don't know why I'm complaining.

9

What 10-year-old kid doesn't want to spend time in a cemetery taking pictures of rocks with dead people's names carved in them? It fucking sucked. Hey Dad, I'm alive and sitting right next to you, how about you fucking pay attention to me?

By all accounts other than this one, my dad was a pretty terrific guy. As a teacher, I have heard countless stories from his students about how inspirational he was to them. Stories about how he talked to his students about what they were going to do with their lives. He wouldn't just focus on art, but what were they going to do when they left school? As time went on, I got pretty fucking annoyed hearing those stories. Sure, in the moment when people were tearing up about how they loved my dad, I would play along, but inside I was like "that fucker!" Talk to your own kid, bud! They would cause a pit inside my stomach because my dad could have had those conversations with me, and he didn't. I don't know what made me different than these total strangers that he was helping. If he was looking for a kid to help who was struggling, he had one living under the same roof with him.

While my dad was an art teacher, I didn't see him do art or make art, whatever you call it, at home. Our house had many things in it that he created. There were paintings and drawings, and even a charcoal sketch that my dad did of his dad that was stunning. I wish I could have spent that amount of time with my dad to do a charcoal sketch of him. It would have been bad because I am terrible at drawing. The only thing I can draw is a bath. I know that joke sucked, but it seemed like things were getting pretty heavy.

I don't know why my dad didn't draw, or paint, or pot (whatever the verb is for pottery) at home. Looking back, it seemed strange. He seemed to me to be a highly creative person. He would make these things, but I wouldn't see him create. With these other kids and his creations at school, it was as if he had another life where he was doing things that he enjoyed, away from home. It made me feel confused about who my dad really was. I'd hear these stories about how people thought he was great, but I only saw a small part of who he truly was.

My favorite memory of my dad was when I was one of his students. In my senior year, I decided to take Art. I wanted to see how my dad was as a teacher. Also, I was a senior, and I wanted a blow-off class to pad my GPA. Sorry, Dad! It was a blast. I got to experience my dad in a whole new setting. He was a great teacher. If there were kids who wanted to fuck around in his class, he'd let them, but they ran the risk of failing. It's one thing if you failed English, but if you failed Art, that's pretty embarrassing. For the kids who did enjoy the pursuit of Art, he challenged them. It was as if he made a lesson plan for each person and tailored it to how much effort they put in. I was terrible at drawing, but I liked pottery. He showed me some things and how to pot (again, not sure if that's the term).

We also had this great two-man comedy team thing that we'd do. We'd take turns being the straight man and the jokester. The best memory that I have is one day my dad told me in the car on the way to school that if someone ever came to me and asked, "How many pushups can your uncle do?" I was supposed to act devastated and say, "My uncle doesn't have any arms." At the moment, I was like "What the fuck?! This is crazy, Dad." Now, having a son of my own, I deeply appreciate the genius.

The joke paid off beautifully one day in Art class. I was working on some of my self-portraits, which looked like a drunken eight-year-old drew it. As I was contemplating ways I could set my self-portrait on fire and still get credit for the assignment, I overheard my dad ask this girl in my class to come over to his desk. To be honest, this girl was the third reason that I decided to take art because she possessed the physical attributes that appealed to the teenage male, if you know what I mean. By that I mean she had great tits. Anyway, I heard my dad tell her, "Hey, go over there and ask Nick how many pushups his uncle can do." That was my cue. I got in character, and when she came over and awkwardly

11

asked me, "Nick, how many pushups can your uncle do?" I delivered a Meryl Streep-level performance. My punim went from shocked to hurt. My lower lip began to tremble a bit, and I bit it so it would stop moving. I looked into her eyes and said, "My uncle doesn't have any arms." I even doubled down and went off script, "Oh my God, why would you ask me that?" I also threw in a little clutch of the pearls kind of motion. She was devastated, and my dad and I had a good laugh. Maybe that's why she and I never dated in high school? I'm sure it was that and not the fact that I had a haircut that made me look like Moe from The Three Stooges. My dad and I pulled off this little goof a few times after that, but I miss that this is something he and I can never do again. To make up for it, I have taught my son the gag. Julian and I are still waiting for the right victim.

When I was about 10 years old, I discovered that my dad was a fuckin' wizard at video games. Quick flashback - on probably the only trip that my parents ever took without me, they went to California and brought back the first Nintendo. Receiving that Nintendo (with Duck Hunt, I might add) altered the course of my life. It was like handing someone who was predisposed to have addiction issues a garbage bag full of heroin. Now I didn't have to be alone anymore, I could sit for hours in front of a TV and rot my brain with video games. Spoiler alert - I turned out just fine, thank you very much.

What was odd about the Nintendo was that you could tell that someone had been playing with it before they brought it home. There wasn't any styrofoam. When I asked him about it, my dad said that he'd been playing with it before they brought it home. I'm sure that was for quality assurance purposes only.

Having a dad who was good at video games must feel like what it was like to have an older brother that was good at video games, you never got to play. I'd have to wake up pretty early in the morning to beat my dad to the Nintendo so I could play Mario Brothers. I don't remember us playing together very much. I'm not sure if that was by design. He might have been like "this kid sucks at Contra, I don't wanna lose," I'm not sure. I do remember watching him play all the time and asking questions about what he was doing and why he did this move instead of that. Anyone that has asked questions of someone that is playing video games will know you're not going to get a detailed answer, it usually is a simple "yeah" or "nah" or "Come on, I'm playing a game here!"

As I got older, my friends started learning that my dad was a savant with video games. There were times when I would answer the phone, and it was one of my friends who had called. They didn't want to talk to me, though. They asked for my dad. "Hey Nick, I can't get past this level in Zelda. Is your dad around?" Going to find my dad so he could talk to my friend about video games was a weird experience. "Jeff, no games before you finish your homework."

My dad also sold video games out of his classroom at the high school. Yes, you read that correctly. My father, a teacher, sold new and used video games to my fellow students out of his classroom, like the first GameStop. He'd have a list of prices printed out and would distribute them like some sort of black market bodega. Kids would stop by his room in between classes. They'd slip him the cash, and he'd slip them Kid Icarus.

I spent a lot of time with my grandparents. My dad would drop me off at my grandparents' house in Bannister to catch the bus to school, and then I'd ride the bus back to their house after school. I'd stay there with them until my parents would pick me up in the evening. Most of the time I'd eat dinner with my grandparents and we'd watch the old TV shows from the 70s like The Jeffersons or Happy Days.

My dad's parents were amazing people. My grandpa's name was Elmer. You don't hear that name too much anymore, huh? That's because it's pretty weird. He had two nicknames. The first was "Elm," and the second was "Dutch." When your option was being referred to as a deciduous tree or "Dutch," I'd go with

13

Dutch. He had no idea how or why someone started calling him that, but he stuck with it. That's how you know it's a great nickname - you don't know why or how you got it.

He was a veteran of World War II. With a German last name of Leydorf, I should probably mention that he fought for the United States in World War II. He wasn't a Nazi. He was in the military police and fought in Italy and North Africa during the war. When the war was over he landed a pretty sweet position, which was being one of the guards at The Tomb of the Unknown Soldier. The guards have a ceremony that they perform several times a day. It's a very prestigious posting. My grandpa never talked about it. I couldn't imagine the man that used to make me blueberry pancakes every morning before school and lay on his side on the floor after dinner and watch Jeopardy with me held one of the most honored positions in the military. That's how people were back then, I guess. Maybe they would have been different if they had TikTok or Twitter. Maybe my Grandpa Elmer would have tweeted during the war - "Just bagged a Nazi!" Not to be outdone, my uncle, Michael Leydorf, flew the planes that refuel Air Force One. He also didn't talk about it at all. As it turns out, the Leydorf men share similar traits - they are feared by men and loved by women. They also have problems expressing their emotions and suffer from male pattern baldness.

My dad's mother (that's my grandmother if you weren't sure how a family tree works) was named Maxine Leydorf. She was a very cool lady. I am grateful to her for many things. Education was particularly important to her and she made me read for an hour everyday when I came home from school. I couldn't do anything until I did that. If she didn't make me do that, who knows where I would be now - probably wearing a MAGA hat and working at a bowling alley. From ages 8-12, she would take me every Wednesday to the local library in Elsie, Michigan to check out books. I'd read 2-3 per week. It's not like the Elsie Public Library was the National Archives, but they did have a pretty cool

14

collection of books. I read so many of the books that I had to read "The American Girls" books. Until this day, I have never told that to everyone. I made my grandma check them out in her name so as to keep me anonymous. I didn't want my name showing up in the back of the book on the card showing the list of people who checked them out. Although, I am sure they would have figured out that my grandma, a 65 year old woman, wasn't the one that was reading books for young girls.

I gravitated toward Samantha. That's probably because she grew up in a household with her grandma and had no one to play with her. Fuck, that sounds depressing as I write that. It's weird to me that my childhood happened the way it did. I was a pretty cool kid. I didn't smell bad or anything like that, or at least no one told me that I did. Hopefully, the problem was simply growing up in the middle of nowhere. Yeah, I would have distinctly remembered someone say to me "Leydorf, you smell bad." Anyway, there was a dearth of kids to play with and the ones that were cool lived 10 minutes away by car. To a 10 year old, that might as well have been 100 miles away.

Low-Grade Terror

After that douchebag client threatened my life, I just had to go on about my day. There wasn't a news crew or Oprah to help me figure out what to do next. First, I had to get out of the cell that they call an attorney-client visitation room. I forgot that I was locked in, so when I tried to make a grand exit, I was left awkwardly trying to push the door open. I had to push a red button so someone could let me out. I hadn't committed any crimes, so why was I the one who was locked in? Once I pushed it, it seemed like forever until someone figured out that I wanted to leave. With my client and me locked together in this room, there was an incredibly awkward silence.

There was nothing else I could do but just wait there holding my work bag, not looking this guy in the eye. It took forever. I wanted to say, "Hey, this dude just threatened to kill me. Can you hurry the fuck up over there?" I wanted to just keep pushing the button until they let me out, but even in this situation, my midwestern politeness took over, and I didn't want to bother the person whose only fucking job was to let people out of this shitty room. It was the kind of awkward silence after someone just broke up with you, but you were trapped in an elevator, except here, the person who just broke up with you also threatened to kill you.

Waiting, waiting, waiting. Finally, I heard an electronic buzz and a terrible noise, "BHGGHRT." It reminded me of the fire alarm in the trailer where I grew up. That stupid thing would go off when my parents would cook, it would go off when they weren't cooking, it would go off in the summer, and if you farted wrong, it would go off. It would go off for any goddamn reason. It was so jarring for me to hear. I'm positive that it's etched onto my chromosomes. When it buzzed that morning in that attorney-client room, I jumped just like I would when I was a kid.

The door buzzed and vibrated because I had my hand on the handle. I pushed open the door, and a slight breeze pushed against my face from the movement of the door. I walked through the empty room with other chairs and tables bolted to the ground. The lights were so bright and fluorescent that they burned my eyes. I felt like everyone was looking at me, but no one was there. The next door buzzed, and I opened and walked through it. The lady behind the bulletproof glass said, "Have a nice day!" I don't think my mouth made words, but some sounds came out.

I walked out of the main door of the sheriff's department to the parking lot. If this scene were in a movie, the hero would walk out to a Coldplay song and triumphantly drive into the sunset. I stumbled across the empty parking lot, nearly falling on my ass slipping on patches of ice trying to get to my Nissan Altima. I pushed the button on the door to unlock it, but it didn't work. It beeped but didn't work. I repeatedly pulled the door handle out of frustration and mumbled, "Come on!" It finally opened. I threw my briefcase across to the passenger seat. I got in and I sat there and I cried. It was 10:27 am. My phone's Bluetooth synced with my car, and "Ruff Ryder's Anthem" by DMX started playing. Where was DMX when I needed him? I really could have used him in that attorney-client room. He would have yelled some shit at my client, and then I would have "Yeah, that's right!"

I don't know if at any time in human history anyone has ever cried listening to DMX before. If they did, I'm positive it's not because of the beauty of his prose. "Put my shit on tapes / Like you bussin' grapes"? What the fuck does that even mean? I do know that DMX wouldn't have taken that shit if he were a lawyer. It would be wild if DMX were a lawyer to begin with. He would have probably had several interviews with "Character & Fitness."

I know I cried because I had bottled up who I was inside of a suit and tie for 12 years, and I didn't know who I was anymore. The stress, the student loans, the weight of responsibility had changed me and not for the better. I don't remember the drive home. My mind was racing as I plotted out my next move. Like my lawyer training has taught me, as I drive back to Lansing, my thoughts migrate toward the worst-case scenario. What the fuck am I supposed to do now? What are the legal implications of this? While there were many things that I didn't know, I knew that I didn't want to represent that guy anymore. Even if he called me from jail and was like, "I'm so sorry, boo. You mean the world to me. You know I love you." I would have been like "nah, I'm good. You hurt my feelings, dog."

I didn't run. I just sat there after he said it. I knew what I had to do, but I felt immobilized by fear. I felt like a failure. I thought, "What did I do to make this guy say that he wanted to kill me?" I felt like the mom on Seinfeld when she told Jerry, "How could anyone not like you?" As I sat on the metal stool, it felt cold on my ass. My lawyer pants were very thin, and the cold worked its way through the fabric and met with my ass sweat. In addition to discovering what happens to you when someone threatens your life, that morning I also learned how much your ass sweats when someone threatens your life. It's a lot. Not to get gross, but it's too much sweat to be on your ass.

In a classic brain move, I became hyper-aware of my surroundings. The stool was fixed to the floor and couldn't move, just like me. I also became very aware of the 6-inch gap at the bottom of the fence. There's no reason that they needed that gap because you could send paperwork through it. After all, it's a fence. Here's a suggestion: When you leave a 6-inch gap at the bottom of a fence in a room where lawyers are going to meet with scary people, do the lawyers a solid and add a bottom to the fence! I'm going to find whatever idiot who designed this and threaten to kill them in this room. I'm sure the gap in the bottom of the fence would be fixed by noon. I mean, did they have budget problems? "Hank, if we cut off the bottom of this fence in the attorney-client room, we'll save 73 cents. What do ya' think?"

After he proclaimed that we were not best friends, I wanted to tell this guy to go fuck himself. Over the years, I had built up a reservoir of anger dealing with the worst people. Rude people, energy draining people, and people who were just plain assholes. There were the disappointed, whiny clients who accused me of not doing my job, but before they hired me had completely and stupidly confessed to the police. What the fuck am I supposed to do when you confessed, douchebag? It took so much restraint because in the myriad of conflicting emotions, one choice that I could make was spewing out all of that anger at this guy sitting in a jumpsuit like a firehose, and there was nothing he could do about it. Well, I guess he could try and take a swipe at me through that gap under the stupid fucking fence that they had to divide us.

But I didn't say anything. I just sat there with my sweaty ass and said nothing. I was paralyzed by fear and so many other emotions that I'd never felt in combination before. Like mixing vodka and Coke (the drink, not cocaine) together. I was just a scared 12-year-old boy in a suit and tie in Charlotte, Michigan. I wish that I could have teleported myself back to my childhood room at that minute and played Bulls vs Lakers and The NBA Playoffs on SEGA Genesis. I wish I could have put up the door knob sign with the Tyrannosaurus Rex on it that read "Keep Out - Violators Will Be Eaten." But I couldn't. I had made choices. I had made choices in the choose-your-own-adventure that was my life, and I couldn't flip back and choose again. I had student loans. I had a wife. I had a son. But at that moment, I needed a hug. I wanted to tell that guy to fuck himself for hurting my feelings.

Telling someone that you're going to kill them is a really mean thing to say. I've never threatened anyone's life before, but it's a real dick move. It's one thing to just go off and kill somebody, but it takes a special kind of asshole to threaten someone's life. In passing before he threatened me, he asked me, "Are you still living over on S------ Lane?" I wasn't at the time. That was the place that we just moved from, but I was like, "How the fuck does he know where I live?" Oh yeah, all of your property records are searchable online. Thanks, Al Gore, for your little invention called the internet.

If he knew where I lived, I'm sure he could figure out where I live now. This little piece of information amped up the anxiety for me. Normally, I wouldn't be concerned if an asshole in jail said some bullshit to me, because their ass was in jail. Unless he's digging his ass out of there with a spoon, he's not going to be a threat. However, this asshole knew how the internet worked. He was also in a Chicago-based gang that set up a franchise in mid-Michigan, so he had friends. I would hope that if he was going to do something like that, he wouldn't waste the opportunity on a 30-something bald lawyer who was just trying to help him. However, I've read pages and pages of his convictions, so I had my doubts about his decision-making.

I wanted to tell him, "Go fuck yourself, bud," but I didn't. I regret not doing that. What's bizarre is that what stopped me is that I didn't want him to file a grievance against my license. I didn't want to be a lawyer anymore, but I was concerned that I'd get a blemish on my license. Yeah, that's me. I have a tendency to overthink things. On second thought, I don't think the bar association would discipline me for telling a dude that just threatened to kill me to go fuck himself. Who knows, they've suspended people for less. I don't know what they would have done, but I do know that I regret that decision every day. Maybe after I write this book, I'll visit him and tell him to fuck off.

Why Did I Do This To Myself?

I hated every single second of law school. If I had to choose between doing law school all over again or getting a Trump 2024 face tattoo instead, I'm inking up my face, friend. I'd rather endure 3 weeks of having a frontier dentist fix my overbite than do 3 years of law school again. I'd rather … okay, I think you get it.

After much self-reflection and years of individual therapy, I honestly don't have an answer why I chose to become a lawyer. If there was a gun to my head (I'm not sure why someone would have a gun to my head and demand an answer to that question), I'd say it was because I didn't like to see injustice, watch people suffer, and I really wanted to forcefully say "objection!" in court.

It certainly wasn't because I had experienced what it was going to be like being a lawyer. I grew up in a rural area with two non-lawyer parents. Before I became a lawyer, I didn't know a lawyer. I didn't even meet a real lawyer in person until I went to law school. That's not the norm. I don't think a kid decides to become a cop without at least doing a ride-along and seeing what it's like writing traffic tickets, writing reports, and saying "perp" a lot.

If I had it to do it all over again, I would take 20 minutes to chat with a lawyer and get in early on Bitcoin. If I had taken the time to learn about what a lawyer does beforehand, I'm sure I would have found out that becoming a lawyer fucked them up, and I would have become an architect or something productive. At least I had some experience with building. I mean, I did have a lot of LEGOs growing up. I guess the point I unexpectedly discovered here is that there's no playtime equivalent of what it's like to be a lawyer. There isn't a "Lil' Lawyer Playset" where you can draft your first lawsuit. I don't know how trademark law works, but I'm trademarking this idea. Back off, fuckers, it's mine!

I don't know if I can pinpoint the moment when I made this life-changing decision to become a lawyer, but let's see if talking about high school can shed any light on why I did this to myself, shall we? I don't know why I asked for your permission. This isn't a "choose your own adventure" kind of book. I had that opportunity with my own life and kinda fucked it up by becoming an attorney. *Ouch, Nick, that's harsh.*

Anyway, the first half of high school was life-altering and changed the trajectory of my family. My great-grandfather died. That meant that we could move into his house. Other than my great-grandfather, the only other person whose death I celebrated was Rush Limbaugh. I can feel your judgment, and I don't give a fuck. While he was my great-grandfather, he wasn't a great person. If a kid doesn't like you, you're probably a terrible person. For his sake, I hope all the woo-woo things my wife believes in are true - now he is free of the ego, or whatever, and he is the best version of himself. Honestly, I just hope he stopped saying the n-word. Whether you support my celebration of his death or not, his expiring meant that I didn't have to endure the traumatic sound of the smoke alarm and the chipmunk infestation.

As high school went on, I began to feel comfortable with myself. I started to lose weight, I got contacts, and I touched a boob. It was neat. However, when the topic of what I was going to do after high school came up, I would get nervous and uncomfortable. My insides would start to churn and tighten, like I was about to ask a girl out on a date. I'd get all mumbly and weird.

23

I would just blurt out "I'm going to be a lawyer" when someone's parent would ask what my plans were, and they wouldn't follow up with other questions after that. If they had, I wasn't prepared to answer them. I enjoyed playing video games and playing sports, and music. I did not enjoy talking about what I was going to do after high school.

I was a good student. I graduated 8th in the Ovid Elsie High School Class of 1998. Sure, the school was in the middle of a cornfield, but being 8th out of 180 students was nothing to sneeze at. I had solid extracurriculars: I was in Concert Band, Marching Band, Quiz Bowl, National Honor Society, and some other bullshit things that you could put on your college applications.

I was part of the quiz bowl team that won Quiz Busters that year, a trivia competition on public television, and all of us won a year of free tuition to Michigan State University. Even I, the alternate. That was pretty cool. I won a scholarship, and I wasn't even there for the final game. I probably had some other important shit going on, like jerking off or playing SEGA Genesis. I do remember my dad getting a call when the team got back (because there were no cell phones at the time) with our coach saying that we won. I was pretty stoked about it when I learned that and immediately went back to playing video games. Cool, I thought, at least I know where I'm going to college now. Now back to playing NBA Live '95.

I also liked the idea of going to Michigan State because they didn't require that you take the SAT; you only had to take the ACT. Less work and I don't have to spend time figuring out other alternatives. Umm, yes, please.

I did exactly okay on the ACT. I probably should have retaken it given the fact that I almost died minutes before the test. The morning that I was going to take the ACT, my friend Erin drove us to Alma College in her parents' big fucking truck in the middle of a snowstorm. I hadn't studied at all because no one had told me how important this test might be for your entire future. Our college

24

counselors had more important things to do, like keeping high school kids from fucking. Several girls that year got pregnant and had to go to alternative education.

Should I ultimately be responsible for my own life? Yes. Should someone have at least pulled me aside and talked to me about college applications and the ACT? Yes. Should I stop posing softball questions to myself and answering them? Also yes.

When I say it was a snowstorm, I mean it was a whiteout. We ended up driving off the road. I remember Erin's driving was stellar. The roads hadn't been salted or plowed yet, and the back end of the truck went wonky, and we drove into the median. Luckily, there were no cars on the other side of the road, so Erin did a U-turn on a four-lane highway, and we headed in the opposite direction. Instead of saying fuck it, let's take it again at another time, we still headed up to the testing facility at Alma College. We arrived late and the test had already started. Nothing like showing up late to the most important test you've taken thus far in your life, right? We ran into the testing facility, and everyone was already at work on the exam. All that was missing was a clown who was laughing at my penis, and we would have recreated one of my recurring adolescent nightmares.

Throughout the test, I had so much anxiety that there was a humming in my ears for the entire test. I got the results and they were alright, enough to get into Michigan State. Erin told me her score and did amazing even after cheating death the morning of the test. I was like, "How the fuck did you do that?" At the time, I thought it was part of some evil genius plan to sabotage my success. Erin's now a successful doctor in Oregon, and she's never gone on the record to deny the plot to take me down, but I'll get the truth out of her someday. Someday.

I remember showing my parents what I got on my ACT, and they reacted as they normally did - like the third bowl of porridge. Not too hot, not too cold. Just... nothing. But I craved encouragement. I felt invisible. I could have easily made destructive choices to act out for their attention, but luckily, I chose to pursue accomplishments to get their attention. However, this didn't work either because it led me down an even lonelier road of downplaying my own successes. It's no wonder that burnout was in my future.

On the outside I shrugged it off. But inside, I wanted someone to grab me by the shoulders and say, "This matters. *You* matter. You can do more." Instead, I felt like I was floating through my own future without an anchor, making decisions that felt as random as rolling dice. Their non-reaction became my reaction—I learned to act like my achievements and failures didn't matter either. And if you do that long enough, you start to believe it.

I felt disappointed that I didn't do as well as I had hoped, and they came across like it didn't matter too much. This same attitude would continue to present itself as I moved on to bigger and more life-changing decisions. It was as if they hadn't had to make these kinds of decisions with college before, so they had no idea what to say or how to act. A "don't worry, honey, you can take it again and we'll drive you" would have gone a long way. As a parent myself now, it seems like you have to get involved with your kid's career choices 3 minutes after they're shot out of your wife's vagina. If you haven't already filled out applications for the top 3 preschools in the area, you should be worried that your kid is going to be a dunder/doofus hybrid.

Feeling safe from the lukewarm response I received from my two important authority figures, I continued down the path of attending Michigan State. As things did go on, I did receive a few letters from some schools that I had never heard of before asking me to play sports at their school. One was from a school in Illinois, and they wanted me to come play baseball for them. Had they seen me play? They must not have seen me pitch, or field, or hit. They didn't hear about the 9-run first inning against Owosso, where I didn't get anyone out, and when I was walking back to the dugout, I threw my glove out of the park. It was the 4th thing that I had a

26

part of, leaving the field that afternoon - one glove and three home runs.

As far as football goes, I had only played one year, my senior year. I tried out my freshman year and quit after two days because I hadn't gotten in shape. You'd think that my dad would have said, "Isn't football coming up? You should probably start running to get in shape." I had no fucking clue what was going to happen, and the two-a-day practices chewed me up and spit me out. I decided to stick it out in my senior year. I wanted to do it as a challenge to myself.

I had been cut from the basketball team my junior year when there was a coaching change. A coach who had won a state championship at a smaller school had moved to our school and was going to become the new vice principal. Up until that point, basketball was what I loved the most. I played it all the time. I was on every team from 6th grade up until 10th grade. Then this new coach came in and had no idea about who the players were who had been showing up early and staying late for practice all of these years.

On the 3rd day of practice, I suffered a terrible high-ankle sprain. I could barely walk and couldn't practice at all the rest of the week of tryouts. That Friday, he called me into his office during the middle of the day and cut me.

I cried for hours. Not just because basketball was gone, but because it felt like *I* was gone. For years, the game had been the one place I could forget Bannister, forget loneliness, forget feeling invisible at home. Basketball was the one thing that made me feel valuable. And in one conversation, it was ripped away.

I cried during my final exams, and sometimes just out of the blue it would hit me and I'd tear up. Oh yeah, I forgot to mention that. He cut me on the day of final exams. It wasn't just teenage drama tears — it was grief. I didn't have the language for it then, but I felt worthless. The message I heard was: *you're not good enough, and you never will be.* And a piece of me believed it.

To my credit, when he cut me, he said, "I may be making a huge mistake," and I told him, "Yes, you are." But inside I wasn't so sure. Inside, I felt small. It's funny, now, to say the team didn't win 2 games that season, but back then I would have given anything to be out there losing with them instead of sitting alone, replaying the moment he told me I wasn't wanted. I don't think the team won 2 games that entire season. I was devastated, and I wanted to get in much better shape. I did and then decided to try out for the football team.

Getting cut from the basketball team was humiliating because sports had been a part of my identity and some prick told me that part wasn't good enough. It made me angrier and reinforced the belief that I wasn't good enough. It pushed me harder to seek validation elsewhere, so I turned to a new thing to get attention and stand out.

I had never played organized football before, but I knew how the game was played because I was a white kid from the Midwest. After spending a summer working out with some of the guys on the team, I felt that I was ready for practice. I wasn't disillusioned. I knew that I was going to have my ass handed to me, but there would be a little less of my ass because I had been running stairs and lifting weights over the summer.

The first day of practice came, and to my surprise, it wasn't that difficult. I was looking around like, "Is this it?" Then we had a scrimmage. Wait, this is fun, I thought. I hadn't played a down of organized football, but my friend Brad pulled me in and lined me up at defensive end. I had no fucking clue what to do. I had only played Madden before, and I was able to switch between players on defense.

The offense lined up in the Ovid Elsie patented Wing-T formation. If you don't know what the Wing-T is, it's the offense that teams ran before the invention of the forward pass. You know, when you see black and white movies of football, when guys had no facemasks? The Wing-T is the offense that they were running.

There are two tight ends and three running backs with no wide receivers. Our team ran the ball 95% of the time.

I lined up at left outside linebacker. I was scared shitless. The quarterback hiked the ball and handed it to one of the three running backs in the backfield. A lane opened up, and I shed my blocker and moved into that lane and destroyed the running back. I didn't tackle him; he just ran into me and fell. It felt like a video game kind of hit. The kid was on his back on the ground. A primal yell came out of my mouth like I just killed a deer with my bare hands. Everyone fell silent like, "Where the fuck has this guy been for 4 years?"

That was probably one of the best moments of my football career. For some reason that I didn't understand, they put me with the offensive linemen and defensive linemen to practice. I hated offensive line. I was last in the pecking order of those two groups, and it seemed like unimaginative work. Block this guy. Next play, you're going to change things up and block that guy.

After a quarter of the season had passed and we had lost every game, the coach called me into his classroom one afternoon. He was from the Upper Peninsula of Michigan and was a very unpredictable guy. If you're not from Michigan, the Upper Peninsula isn't the part of the hand; it's the thing that is up above the hand. There's not a lot going on up there. There are a bunch of Native American casinos and snow.

My football coach was also my history teacher for this class I took on the American civil war. It was weird seeing a guy scream at everyone for hours on the football field if they missed a block and then watch him cry when he talked about when Joshua Lawrence Chamberlain ordered his soldiers to affix bayonets when they ran out of ammo at the Battle of Gettysburg.

When he called me in, I had no idea whether he was going to yell at me or cry. Fortunately, it was neither. He complimented me on my effort through summer two-a-days and so far through the season. While I appreciated the compliment and was enamored by

29

his Yooper accent (that's what we call people from the Upper Peninsula), I had a sneaking suspicion: *He's going to cut me from the team. Goddamn it, I can't get cut from another team!* To my surprise, he said, "Nicky, you're too good an athlete to be playing offensive line," and he wanted to move me to tight end. Thank you, Jesus! I was so relieved. I was envious of the tight ends in practice because they got to touch a football. What they were doing looked like a goddamn pleasure cruise compared to rolling around with other dudes on the ground.

I never ended up playing much, but I had a lot of fun. I was a scout team tight end. It sounds like I was a spy. Unfortunately, it didn't require the use of any covert ops or clandestine tradecraft. The scout team played the role of the offense of the team that we were going to play that week. We'd run their offense against our starting defense. That was a weird dynamic. If you did well, your friends were going to get yelled at because the backups were beating you playing an offense that they learned five minutes ago. I enjoyed it.

I like the strategy of football. I wasn't getting my fill playing offensive line, so I looked forward to it. Also, considering that I never received a playbook for our turn of the 18th-century offense, calling plays that were developed after the invention of the forward pass was enjoyable.

One week, we were going to play a team that had an amazing tight end. It ended up being the most fun I ever had during my brief football career. It was my job to be that amazing tight end. All of my teammates had years of football experience. I just switched positions two weeks ago, having never played organized football before. I had the ball thrown to me all week during practice. My basketball experience kicked in, and I never dropped a pass. I made great catches, I broke tackles, I scored touchdowns. It felt amazing. I remember one catch I made over the middle during practice. The ball was thrown over the middle, and I was going to take a big hit if I was going to catch this ball. The safety

30

was getting ready to put a big hit on me. However, I was 6'4" and 250 pounds, and this kid was not. He bounced off of me like I was wearing one of those inflatable sumo wrestling suits. It was one of those hits where you hear everyone on the sideline say "ohhhhh."

In another play, I made a great catch, headed upfield, and dragged a kid until the coach blew the whistle. However, I did feel bad that my friends were getting their ass chewed out by the defensive coaches. "If Leydorf has never played football and he's kicking your ass, how do you think we're going to do on Friday night?"

Over the season, I was awarded scout player of the week a few times. I ended up becoming a special-teams player, and that was fun. At the end of the year, I was selected most improved player. Honestly, I should have won that anyway because I was pretty fucking terrible and I became a decent player by the end of the year.

Playing just that one year of football taught me that I could do anything. It wasn't just physical, it was mental. I had no idea what a tight end should do once the ball is snapped, but I learned. I had no idea what our playbook was, but I learned (honestly, it wasn't that difficult - we ran the ball like every play). Three years before, I had quit the team after the first day of practice, and that stuck with me. To me, it was a failure. While no one probably ever remembered me quitting but me, it was something that I wanted to correct. A few years later, I did.

Your Client Threatens
to Kill You, Now What?

I had to figure out what to do. In times of fear, I think people revert to their old patterns, and that's what I did. I started the operating sequence named "Total Emotional Shutdown." I kept it all inside. Don't ask for help. You're a lawyer. You can think your way out of this. So, I did what anyone would do in that situation: I Googled "what to do when your client threatens to kill you." I felt a tiny wave of reassurance wash over me. "Someone else has been through this before," I thought. On the first page, I found a law review article. Good! This was written by a lawyer. They'll know exactly what to do.

Here's the thing about law review articles that I should have known. I don't know why I thought I'd get a warm blanket of hope wrapped around me from a law review article, but I guess that's how desperate I was. They're written by law robots. Not AI robots. People who are trained as lawyers who are devoid of feelings. There's not one ounce of humanness in a law review article. It's "the Supreme Court said this. The model rules of professional conduct said that. Beep-borp. Laws." I read it and felt no better than I did when those words left my client's stupid mouth. I did, however, feel like taking a big ol' nap like the ones after Thanksgiving dinner because it was one of the Top 47 most boring things I've ever read. Leave it to a boring ass lawyer to take an emotionally charged situation chock-full of layers and the opportunity for narrative and make it boring as fuck. I was on law review in law school, so I should have known about law review articles being drier than an insurance seminar. I can tell you that being on law review was like working in a sweatshop without the iPhones. I spent a year of my life working long hours for free. I was working on someone else's life's work, one painstakingly boring sentence at a time. My goddamn name better be on a volume or two, but I've never taken the time to check. They gave me a plaque saying I achieved something but so did graduates from Trump University.

I sat in my office for an hour and unsuccessfully tried to go about my day. My phone rang. I ignored it. I checked my email and deleted my spam folder. I get a lot of spam emails. It's annoying. But you know what? It's not as annoying as someone threatening to kill you when you can lose your license if you tell them to go fuck themselves!

I felt the pressure to stay on this case. The circuit court judge who was presiding over this case had their assistant reach out and see if I was available to take this case. When I received that email, I felt proud. I felt honored to take this case on. At the time, I had no idea that this case would be a turning point in my life, and it would consume all of my time and end up with me appearing in a hearing, artfully trying to tell the judge that I could no longer represent this client because there had been a "communication breakdown." Insert Led Zeppelin reference here.

Honestly, if I had known all of that, I probably wouldn't have taken the case, but this needed to happen for me. I needed to get my shit together, and sometimes you need a blow to the head to wake you up out of a funk. The case was handled by a younger prosecutor, Billy. He is a nice person, but he was also a prosecutor.

I mean that with as much respect as possible. It's a difficult job. However, there are a lot of shitbag prosecutors out there. Prosecutors who you wouldn't want to handle a parking ticket, let alone if someone broke into your house and stole your shit. Just Google overzealous prosecutors or open Netflix and you can learn about how the unquenchable thirst for power and promotion can drive otherwise good people to do terrible things and try to cover them up.

I believe this was Billy's first capital case. Because I took this case over after the preliminary hearing (it's a hearing to determine whether there's enough evidence for trial), Billy didn't know what my strategy would be. He probably also thought, like I did, what defendant is going to want to go to trial on a case where the other 4 people confessed and said you were also there? Not many. But I think he underestimated my client. I know I did. I definitely would have taken a deal under those circumstances. The likelihood of winning at trial is small, but there's a 100% guarantee that you'd get out of prison. Even if I was innocent, I'd consider taking a deal. If you win, you're free to go do whatever you want - except for murder someone. However, if you lose, then that's a wrap, dawg. Cue the sad trombone. Bye, Felicia.

As we got closer to the trial, my anxiety really ramped up. On a scale of 1 to 10, I normally operate around a 6. As the trial grew closer and closer, I was at an 8 on a daily basis. I was irritated at people. I had a short temper with my family, even more than normal. Trivial things would set me off like my wife would move my keys and wallet and I'd act like she took a shit on the hood of my Nissan. I can tell you this, I was pretty fucking stressed out. When I get stressed out, I get irritated. It usually starts with sarcasm. Like "oh, that's nice" when someone cuts me off in traffic. Then I usually shut down and don't want to communicate. My wife wants to talk about everyday stuff and I can't handle it. All she wants to do is talk about going on a day trip and I turn into 10 year old me who wants to do nothing but play video games in my room. I don't want to talk about going to Lake Michigan, I want to sit in my room and play NBA Live '95 on my SEGA Genesis.

There were days that I'd just sit in my office and think. Not doing anything in particular, just thinking. If I went to the bathroom in public, I'd sit on the toilet (because I sit down to pee like a man, dammit) for too long and the automatic timers on the lights would go off. Time would pass as I'd play out different scenarios in my head. My mind can be a dangerous place. No one's safe. It's like John Locke's state of nature up there. The worst thing happens every time. It sounds crazy as I'm writing this, but I would gravitate to the worst possible outcome. I'd do something to fuck up the trial that would end with a very public humiliation for me and then for good measure I'd lose my license to practice law, and my family would be put out into the street.

When the stress piles up, I look for ways to get out my frustration. I feel like I should be doing nothing other than work because a man's life is on the line, so I don't deserve to enjoy my time. Then on the other end, the guy in control of the fun part of my brain is like "what the hell is going on over there? We need a goddamn break! I know a buddy and they unionized and got breaks!" You get the point. It's wild.

While I've always dealt with a lot of stress since becoming a lawyer, this was different. This was the most stress I'd ever dealt with in my life. It even manifested itself into my body. I got the gout. If you don't know what gout is, ask your meemaw. It's why her foot hurts and why if you rub it after Thanksgiving dinner she'll give you a quarter. I'm not a goddamn gout doctor, but it has to do with uric acid building up in your body. Stress can increase production of that acid and that acid forms crystals, not the cool spiritual crystals like labradorite that help with your root chakra. These crystals form in your joints and when you move them it hurts like a motherfucker. Gout comes in attacks. Things will be fine until you have a gout attack and then you're yelling for your mommy because it hurts so bad. During a gout attack my big toe (usually on my right foot because that's my "gout toe") will swell up and get red. It gets so big that it's like it's going to give birth to baby toes like a Twilight Zone episode or something. The only thing that I've found that makes the pain go away immediately is black tar heroin. Sorry, that's a joke. I had to squeeze one in there, all this gout talk was getting depressing.

The only thing that makes the pain go away immediately is hardcore pain meds. But these days, doctors don't wanna just go giving out oxy when some dude comes in saying that his foot hurts. "Here's an Advil. Stop drinking beer and eating pork, fatty." What the fuck?! How am I supposed to live, Doc? Take the foot. Saw it off now like a civil war physician.

In addition to the gout making me feel like an old man, my work- related stress also manifested itself in other ways. Like my right eye started twitching back in 2008. In fact, it's twitching now, just for old times sake. It's pretty annoying. It's like my body is using my right eye to try and communicate with me using morse code. C-H-I-L-L space O-U-T. The only way that I've been able to make it stop is with alcohol. But if I drink alcohol, then it makes my gout worse. It's a vicious cycle.

So, I was really a mess before this trial. I'm hobbling around with my gout toe and my eye is tweaking more than Jesse Pinkman at an NA meeting. If you don't get that reference, you really need to watch Breaking Bad. You're probably missing out on a bunch of Breaking Bad references and a ton of other pop culture references at parties. On the outside it looked funny, almost sitcom-worthy: "lawyer's body falls apart before trial." But inside, it felt like my body was screaming truths I wouldn't say out loud. That I was drowning. That I had no business carrying this much weight. Every twitch of my eye was a Morse code message I couldn't decipher, except that it spelled out one word over and over: *quit.*

The shame of it was brutal. I couldn't tell my wife I was terrified of failing. I couldn't tell my son that Dad was too stressed

36

to be present. So, I sat in silence, pretending it was normal to break down while holding someone else's life in my hands.

Rugby? What the Fuck is Rugby?

After high school, I left the pleasures and splendor that Bannister had to offer and embarked upon a new adventure in East Lansing at Michigan State University. I was big man on campus. I had a quiz bowl scholarship. Form an orderly line, ladies. There's enough of me to go 'round. Even though I was a scholarship athlete, I yearned for sports.

Playing a year of football put me in surprisingly good shape, and I continued that throughout the rest of my senior year. I entered my freshman year at MSU in relatively decent shape. That year, I worked at a 24-hour Gold's Gym on Hagadorn Road. I worked the midnight to 5 am shift. To stay awake, I'd lift weights. One morning, on the gym wall while I was pretending to work, I saw a flyer for the rugby team. I had a vague idea what rugby was because YouTube wasn't really a thing then. I knew that it was a physical game and Australians did it, so it must be an enjoyable time. I didn't want to stop playing sports. Turns out I loved it. You're telling me I can tackle someone without a helmet or pads? Umm, yeah, I'm in.

I had to overcome one obstacle; however, I had no clue how to play. Truth be told, I barely understand the game now, even though I played at Michigan State. I don't think that's a result of the multiple concussions either. It is so goddamn confusing. This is a scrum, this is a ruck. Whatever. How about I just tackle the person with the ball? Turns out that was an effective strategy. I was able to touch the ball more in one rugby game than I ever did in an entire year of high school football. It felt good to tackle people. I wish it were socially acceptable to do it in public. If someone wronged you, you should be able to get down in a three-point stance and level their ass. It seems fair to me.

There are no pads or helmets in rugby. People think that's crazy, but having played both sports, I can tell you that playing without a helmet and pads is a great idea. I know that sounds crazy. But the problem with football is you have 22 genetic freaks of nature on the field at the same time, and they have so many pads on that their bodies are like cinder blocks being thrown around. Players have helmets on, too, so there's no reason to stop you from really getting in there and destroying someone. Rugby is different. You don't have a helmet or pads so you're limited by what your brain tells you is acceptable. There's no padding to add to your mass. There's no helmet to protect your brain, so you're going to be more careful.

It's not like rugby players aren't as athletic as football players, either. Rugby is basically football and soccer mixed together. With football, there's a play that lasts a few seconds, and the whistle is blown. With rugby, the game keeps moving and moving and moving. By the end of the game, you will have run 6 to 7 miles or even more, depending on your position.

At Michigan State, rugby was a club sport. However, don't tell that to the rugby guys I played with. There were some real badasses in the best shape I've ever seen. I had to get in shape real quick. Practices were long and rough. There weren't any breaks. We did way more running than I ever did at football practice. Also, since I had no idea how to play, I was physically and mentally drained by the end of practice. Then I would have to walk back to Holden Hall, which was about a mile away. When I came back from my first practice, my roommate, Roger, asked me if I had been dragged behind a truck. It felt like it.

The games were really fun to watch. Rugby is like hockey on grass. It's fast-paced, and there's going to be a fist-fight. We had three teams: an A team, a B team, and a C team. Even though I had no clue how to play rugby, I was put on the B team. I was cool with that. I was physically bigger than most of the A-team guys, but what they were doing out there far surpassed my knowledge. In the scrum, which is the thing you see in rugby where the ball is rolled on the ground between two groups of players that mash themselves together, I played in the second row. The scrum is a fascinating concept. It takes complete unison of all of the players involved to make it work. If one jackass isn't doing what they're supposed to be doing, their side is going to either commit a penalty or they're going to get moved around by the other team. There's no hiding in a scrum. The team has to play together. There was a lot of yelling amongst each other on the team if someone wasn't doing their part. Sometimes it was me. I wasn't trying to half-ass it; sometimes I had no idea what the fuck was going on.

The second row is an interesting position to play. You basically take your head and put it between the two players directly in front of you, and you're leaning forward into them. You're almost horizontal. A side view of the scrum looks like something you'd see in that "Human Centipede" movie, but I assure you, there was no butt stuff going on. Not that there's anything wrong with that. The taller players usually play this position because they're able to have more leverage to be able to push the players in front of them forward. There are two players in the second row, and they bind themselves together or lock themselves together. Thank you for coming to my TED talk on rugby.

We practiced a couple of times per week, and the games were on Saturday morning. I had 14 credits in my first semester. School and rugby were enough for me. I had always been a great student, and college was no different. In my four years at MSU, I missed probably 2 classes, both because I was too hungover to go to class. A lot of my friends would skip classes. Growing up in a trailer really motivated me to go to class and learn. *I don't want to live in a house that moves again.* My college roommate's go-to quote was "you don't have to go to class!" He was and still is a great dude. A terrible student our first year together, but a good egg. He'd stay up to all hours of the night playing video games, but I was so exhausted I could have fallen asleep in a sawmill.

After the games, there was one common thing that all the rugby players did. Drink. I'm talking alcohol here, not smoothies. Maybe it was just me, but I didn't feel like getting smashed after I ran 7 miles while playing human pinball. On top of being amazing athletes, the A team guys could drink. At our first home game, I discovered that the guys hid a keg of beer in a trash can. Jesus, fellas. Never underestimate the ingenuity of a bunch of alphas that want to drink a few bowls of loudmouth soup. I hope all of them are okay now.

Rugby practices were rough. I remember this one Asian kid who spoke no English who was on the C team. He played rugby back in Singapore. Apparently, it was a different kind of rugby because the first week, he took a hit and went down like a rag doll. Like one of those hits you'll see in a video someone will share with you that you see and are like "Oooooh damn." They had to call the ambulance to pick him up. On the bright side, practice ended early that day. To my surprise, he was back on Saturday for the game. However, he left early when the ambulance came and they carted him off the field. We never saw him again.

I, too, fell victim to injuries from rugby, but they were my fault. By injuries, I'm not talking about the abuse my liver suffered. I think that's implied. I have gout now, but I think that's because I'm German and we eat parts of the animal that should be thrown away and give you gout if you eat them.

One important thing to know about rugby is what to do in the scrum. My position required me to put my head between two other people's bodies. It's hard to explain, so just Google it. I know that's probably not something you'd expect a writer to say, but I don't want to spend five pages describing what a scrum is or how weird it looks. From the side, it looks like some Human Centipede shit. Anyway, I had no clue what I was doing, so one time during practice, we were working on the scrum and it got loose, and my head slipped down between the two hips of the guys in front of me, and then my head was crushed in between them. As it was happening, I was trying to yell for it to stop, but when you're one giant pile of humanity, it's hard to hear someone yelling. The whistle blew, and I fell on my face in the dirt. I lay there for a minute. There was a ringing in my ears that wouldn't go away. My head hurt to the point that it made my eyes squint. I felt scared because I only have one brain. My teammates said I was fine, and it's happened to them before, so I took a minute and went back in, still feeling like what it was like to have my brain put in a vise. I'm not sure why I listened to those animals. If this happened today, I would have been taken to the emergency room like that one Singaporean kid. Instead, I got the typical alpha male response of "you're fine, just rub some dirt on it."

As I rode my bike back to my dorm, it felt like something wasn't right. The ringing was still there, and my eyes hurt. It felt like they were really big inside my head, and I had a headache. I crawled into my bed and went to sleep. I slept for 10 hours and I woke up with a terrible headache again. Even though the lights weren't on, the room was so bright it was unbearable.

That day, I did what no man in my family had ever done before: I went to the doctor. Gasp. I have no idea what it's like now, but Olin was the student health facility at MSU. It wasn't that great. Many of the people who worked there were med students just starting out, so the quality of care wasn't stellar. The story you'd always hear from female friends who went to Olin when they weren't feeling well was that they were asked if they were having their period. If not, then they were given a pregnancy test. When I walked in, it looked like the kind of medical facility you'd see in communist Russia. The fluorescent lights made a hissing noise. They also made everything look strange and drab. I thought someone was going to steal my jeans when I was in the exam room.

My name was called, and I saw a male doctor who looked no older than me. That was unnerving because I looked like a toddler back then. I told him what happened, and he confirmed what I had figured out by looking on WebMD, that I had a concussion. I'm fairly sure he looked up my symptoms on WebMD, too. After we determined that I wasn't having my period and I failed the pregnancy test, I went back to my dorm. This kid, who looked younger than me, said there wasn't much I could do but rest. I had no problem with that. Then he told me that I had to not drink too much alcohol for a couple of weeks. Jesus doc, what are you trying to do, kill me? I squinted from the bright lights and reluctantly agreed to abstain from overly imbibing on alcohol.

Luckily, we didn't have a game that weekend, so I was able to take a break. I was back at it the next week, and the same fucking thing happened again. This time it was worse. The brightness, the headache, everything. I didn't need Doogie Houser, MD, to tell me that I had suffered another concussion. I had been concussed. It was unsettling. There were things I did that week that I had forgotten I had done. My roommate, who at the time was the biggest slob on the planet, was even concerned for my safety. We would often communicate just by using the word "dude" with different inflections. When I went to do my laundry for the second time that day, he responded with a concerned "dude."

I finished the season and went back to Bannister for a couple of weeks. I had told my mom what happened, and in typical mom fashion, she yelled, "Oh my God!" She was probably right. I only had one brain, and I need to keep this one from being ruined by smashing into other guys a few times per week. There was no way I was going to play professional rugby; I didn't even know that existed. I was planning on going to law school, and from what I'd heard, I needed a fully intact brain to complete that. You would have thought that two concussions would have been enough for me to decide that law school was a mistake. But alas, it wasn't. Maybe I should have kept playing, because third time's a charm, right?

Panic

One Sunday afternoon before the trial, I snapped. My body and mind had both reached their breaking points and I started freaking out. I started breathing quicker, like when I used to run, not marathons or anything, just the simplest act that could be described as running. Even though I was breathing quickly, it felt like I wasn't taking in much oxygen. Things got dizzy. I got tunnel vision. I think it was a full-blown panic attack. Luckily, the attorney who owns the building where my office is was upstairs in his office. His name is Nick too. Fair warning, it can get kind of confusing with two Nicks in this part of the story. Just know that I haven't completely flipped out and started referring to myself in the third person like Kanye West or Kenny Banya did in that Seinfeld episode.

I walked up the stairs of the old house that's now our office to see if Nick was there. This place was built in the 1800s so it has a lot of character, which is a euphemism for run down. The building is like when you run into someone who you can tell was really attractive but they got old. The structure was there, but things are falling apart. The railing to the stairs is purely ceremonial in nature, so as I walked up the stairs I was really looking for support. Luckily, Nick was up in his office. I knocked on the door, he said "come in," and I walked in. I must have looked like a complete wreck. I'm sure Nick was regretting saying "come in," but it was a Sunday in the middle of winter in Michigan, so it's not like I was taking him away from watching the Detroit Lions do anything productive.

Nick has been a lawyer for many years. He was also in the military and was a cop. Honestly, the guy is a badass. If I ever decide to go on a crime-spree, Nick is the person that I'd hire to be my lawyer. When I refer people to Nick, I say that and they usually end up hiring him because that's a great recommendation. "He's the guy I'd hire if I ever did some fucked up shit! Five stars!" Boom, you're gonna hire that guy.

I walked in his office and cleared off a chair, because when you're a good lawyer, your office looks like a paper bomb exploded. I sat down and vomited everything that was going on. I talked about my client not wanting to take the deal. The prosecutor not offering my client anything other than 25 years and the possibility of parole. I talked about all of the snitch-ass co-defendants saying my client was there. Nick just sat there expressionless. In my mind, I was kind of just hoping he'd take the whole thing over from me. In a perfect world, he'd just look at his calendar and say "No worries, mate, I can take this over for ya'" I should mention that Nick is NOT Australian. That last quote of him in my dream sequence makes him sound Australian, but he is not.

As I spewed out this story, I started to talk about how much pressure I was feeling and I started to cry. I'd never felt that vulnerable in front of another lawyer before, so that should tell you how low I was feeling. Of all the professions that I wouldn't want to cry in front of, it's probably lawyers because they get paid by the hour to listen to you cry. This profession had turned me into a 37 year old man crying in another man's office. Normally, I'd go home and get irritated with something that my wife did "why did you move my socks, dammit!! Are you trying to sabotage me, woman!" But I didn't have time for putting on a strong public persona. I needed emotional triage immediately and Nick was the on-call resident.

The way he responded is the wonderful thing about Nick. He's the total opposite of me. When there's a stressful situation, I react emotionally and flip out every single time. That's a good trait if you're a professional wrestler, but not when you're a lawyer. I can't be like Macho Man Randy Savage in the courtroom, "Oooh yeah, I can't wait to put you down in the steel cage at trial this coming Monday morning at 9am." That's my first response, but not Nick. He's been there before. He's in his 60s and he's dealt with way more serious shit than I have and he acts like couldn't give a fuck.

He sketched out a blueprint with words of what I should do next. All the while he's citing rules and codes of ethics and procedure and inside I'm saying "damn, he's good." Then he gave me the most important piece of advice, which was that I needed to step back for a minute and chill the fuck out. "Go for a walk." "You're taking this too personally." "Look at it this way, if there's zero chance you're going to win, then what do you have to lose?" It helped. He's given me the same pep talk at various stages since that one. He'll see me coming and I'm sure he's like "oh shit, he's gonna cry again, isn't he?" My point is that I have a ridiculously small number of lawyers that I look up to and Nick is one of them.

They don't teach you about stress management in law school and they should. The entire process of law school is a pressure cooker designed to see whether you can make it out. When you're in the shit, you have no idea what's going on and you're just trying to survive. I know it sounds like I'm trying to make it sound like the Mekong Delta in 1968, but I'm not. I understand that it's just law school. In the movie "Catch Me If You Can" Christopher Walken's character tells everyone a story when he wins an award. It went: "Two little mice fell into a bucket of cream. The first mouse quickly gave up and drowned. The second mouse wouldn't quit. He struggled so hard that eventually he churned that cream into butter and crawled out. Gentlemen, as of this moment, I am that second mouse." That scene is great for two reasons. First, it's fucking Christopher Walken. He's so strangely brilliant "I got a fever and the prescription is more cowbell." No one else could have delivered that line in that SNL sketch like he did. If you don't know what I'm talking about, I'm not mad. I'm confused how you've made it this far. So put this book down and Google "more cowbell." Watch that sketch and then come back. I'll wait. And second, that quote succinctly describes law school.

"What's your point, Nick?" Excellent question, imaginary critic. My point is that there's no fucking reason why it has to be like that. In terms of law school, when those little two mice fell into the bucket of cream, several other mice were there and should have helped both of their dumb asses. But no, law school was a nearly impossible journey. It didn't need to be impossible though. They always tell you that they are trying to teach you to think like a lawyer. However, the way that they're doing it is all wrong. There's no correlation between the process and the end result. That's like if the Marines put their new recruits through all of the misery of basic training and then when they were all done they were like "Okay, now make me a sandwich."

The LSAT
(and What Was Left of My Self-Esteem)

As college moved on, I had a lot of fun. I was drinking on the weekends, playing a lot of video games and having sex with someone other than myself on a regular basis. As I got further in my college career, I did the typical Nick Leydorf move and decided to turn inward, rather than outward. Other people were joining groups and societies. I tried being in one group but it involved my brain being smushed. So I decided to go at college alone.

I did have one great friend, Jon, who was the same major that I was. We met after our senior year of high school, before college started. I was a teller at his credit union and he came in and we hit it off. From the sounds of it, you'd be expecting that we blew each other behind the dumpster of the credit union but it wasn't like that, I swear. We shared a lot of the same opinions about things and it turned out we were going into the same major at Michigan State and were both going to be starting in the fall. I made a friend.

As time progressed, we had many of the same classes together. I'd go religiously and as time went on, Jon religiously wouldn't. He'd ask for my notes because I tended to write everything down and I would reluctantly give them up. When we weren't drinking or watching football or doing the typical things that college guys did, we'd talk about being lawyers and working together. It was exciting to have someone else that was on a similar path. I didn't know any lawyers and he knew a couple. I felt a sense of togetherness that we would be working toward the same goal.

As time went on, Jon discovered that he wasn't going to classes because he discovered that he didn't want to be a lawyer. When he told me he was going to change his major I felt alone. Before he figured this out, we were going to have our own practice and get drunk and do dumb shit forever. Now, I felt like it was just me. I didn't know anyone else in my classes, but I kind of liked it that way.

There was nothing more annoying to me than the stupid shit that some of my cohorts would say out loud in a group of people. What some of my clients would describe as "some ignorant ass bullshit." For instance, one 8am during a large lecture class on the first day of the semester, the professor who had a Boston accent and was wearing a tweed coat with an ascot, I shit you not, he was and he looked every bit as ridiculous as you're picturing him in your head right now. Anyway, this girl who sat right up front raised her arm and it looked as if it was 10 feet tall. She had the longest arm I had ever seen. It was so pronounced because no one else was raising their hand because it was the end of class and we all wanted to get the fuck out of there. The professor says "does anyone have any questions before we leave?" Ms. Longarms gets a wild hair up her ass and extends the pole that is her right phalange. Bobby Boston professor who was probably smoking a pipe at this point to be more on-brand calls on her and she says in a room of about 200 college kids at 8am "Yes, I have a question. Pepsi or Coke?" At that moment, I wanted to break off said arm and insert it her left ear and spear her arm into the ground as a message to all those fucking idiots who would raise their hands in class with stupid fucking questions. She's probably a magistrate or some other noble person now so good for her.

Other jackasses would use the classroom as a means to try out their half thought out bullshit opinions, like some goddamn open mic. It seemed like every class I would have would devolve into a jam session for what would become the alt-right. It only took one look from me at the beginning of the semester to figure out what a person's agenda was going to be for the semester. Oh, this guy hates abortion. This girl thinks that Jimmy Carter was a communist plant. Unexpectedly, one guy would insert how the US fucked up Panama. I'm sure it was true, but at an 8am Political Theory class I didn't give a fuck. I was paying a professor to tell me what they knew, I wasn't interested in the opinion of some twenty year old from Gross Pointe who knows the lyrics to every Rage Against the Machine song. If everyone could shut their fucking mouth, it would be great. It was probably because Facebook wasn't a thing back then. Now you have every opportunity to throw out your half baked opinion on the Illuminati and the patriarchy and it doesn't keep you longer in class.

Looking back, I long for those times. The times before law school. The times before the LSAT. The times when I thought of myself as a pretty intelligent individual. The LSAT changed all of that. If you don't know what the LSAT is, then God has truly blessed you. The LSAT stands for Law School Admissions Test. It's not an interesting acronym really. However, the LSAT also symbolizes the destruction of my self-esteem. When I was a wee lad, the LSAT was required of everyone that wanted to go to law school. As I write this, there is talk of doing away with the LSAT as a requirement in order to get into law school, and to that, I say "that's bullshit," a legal term of art.

Maybe I'm wrong. There are enough people out there who think because they know how to do a Google search, they believe that they're a lawyer. If they didn't have to go to three years of law school and would just have to take the bar exam, maybe they'd crawl back into their hole? Probably not. I'd just like to see them get their comeuppance. I think that's the German in me. Schadenfreude definitely exists inside me and flows through me like the Emperor Palpatine meme that you're probably thinking of now.

Deep down, I am jealous. I'm jealous of them for not having to take that awful exam. At the time, it was the biggest thing in my life. A test that was all multiple choice and lasted a few hours held more weight than all of the hours of classes I'd gone to and the hard work that I'd put in to achieve an excellent undergraduate GPA.

Looking back at it, your LSAT score doesn't mean anything. It's just a way for law schools to sort people into piles. Instead of interviewing you, they can have someone assign you a number based on a multiple-choice exam. It's a lazy way of doing things. It doesn't take into consideration work ethic, desire, or whether or not you're a dickhead. There's no way to test those attributes. What if you had diarrhea? There's no way that you should be judged to be worthy to enter a prestigious law school based on one afternoon of test taking when you ate a bad burrito the night before. I read all these arguments this in book called "Things That People Who Did Terribly on the LSAT Say."

Unfortunately, I tied my self esteem to the result of the LSAT. As far as I was concerned, I didn't do very well, even after two attempts at it. I allowed a three-digit number crush my spirit. I thought my life was over because some doors had closed to the prestigious law schools. It took me well into my mid-thirties to realize that it didn't matter at all. As much as I though it would, the result of one test didn't define me.

I think if the Dalai Lama read this, he would say a few things. "First, you curse too much, Nick." Thanks, Mr. Lama. "Second, you seem to be controlled too much by the ego." You nailed it, Lama. I have lived most of my life ruled by the narrative in my head that says "hey, you should be doing this," and "if you don't

work hard in school, you're going to end up living in a dumpster."
Ego isn't a bad thing, it is something that helps us stay alive.
However, I blindly follow whatever the narrative in my head tells
me to do, to stay moving and working, because the ego tells me if
you don't do these things, you're going to die.

The ego sounds so convincing though. It's your voice telling
you "if you don't send this email, bad things are going to happen."
If it was someone else's voice, say Hugh Grant for example, it'd be
easier to dismiss with a "get out of my head, you limey prick! By
the way, I loved you in Notting Hill." Maybe it's the crystals that
my wife makes me carry around, but as time goes on, I'm coming
to realize that it's me that gets in my own way. It's hard to do
because there's a voice that also says "your amazing!" No matter
how amazing I am, self, I have the sneaking suspicion that I could
have chosen any career and struggled with these areas of my life
like self-esteem. It's just that it took so many hoops to jump
through being a lawyer that it's hard for me to admit that maybe I
made a mistake listening to my ego. "You don't want to end up
poor, do you? You need to be something like a doctor or a
lawyer!" In the U.S., it would be really hard to die from starving to
death. There's always going to be a dumpster behind an Arby's.

Don't Fuck This Up

My trial strategy was simple: don't fucking lose. Actually, it was this - to make the case that the four idiots had "beef" with my client so when they got caught, they wanted a guy they didn't like, my client, to be the one to take the major fall for it. Sounds like the beginning of a rather good Netflix documentary, right?

I spent hours trying to find evidence to fit my theory. For you science nerds out there, I'm sure once you read that you knocked over a beaker or Bunsen burner and yelled "confirmation bias!" But chill the fuck out, Marie Curie. That's the great thing about being a defense lawyer - you don't have to prove ANYTHING. Reasonable doubt is your biggest weapon. Reasonable doubt doesn't mean that you have to have ANY evidence to support your theory. The defendant has a right to present their case after the prosecutor is done, but that rarely happens. The theory goes that the burden on the prosecutor is so high why take a chance and fuck it up if the jury doesn't believe my client's grandma who says "he's a really good boy!"

Obviously, I'm oversimplifying things here. The prosecutor's burden to prove that the defendant is guilty beyond a reasonable doubt is huge. That's why they call it a "burden." With that in mind, if I don't have anything that I can use at trial, it can be a decent strategy to just go up there and raise the question "what if?" in the minds of the jurors. The traditional way of thinking is that the jury is going to be smart enough to see through that. Really? I've seen jurors walk into a glass door before. So I'm not sure the average person is smart enough to figure this out. There is a delicate balance between any doubt and reasonable doubt. There's a line where even the person who drinks from a firehose of conspiracy theory will pause and say "okay, that's bullshit."

Having said that, you'd think that it'd be pretty easy being a defense lawyer. Just throw a bunch of bullshit on the wall, see what sticks, and you're a goddamn hero. Umm, nope. Unfortunately, there's way more to it. It's not what you see on Law and Order. Why do you think lawyers have a reputation for being drunks? It's not all fun and games, Ally McBeal style. There's more to it than the Perry Mason moment when he gets Colonel Mustard on the stand and he breaks under cross examination and says, under oath, that it was indeed him that committed the murder, in the study, with the candlestick. It's dealing with the relentless sea of emotions that people bring to you. A never-ending miasma of anger and frustration. Being charged by the government with a crime stirs a pot of emotion inside of people and I get to deal with the part that boils over.

While I've never been charged with a crime myself, I've been close enough to people that have to see what it can do to them. Whether they did it or they didn't, people are looking for a way to get out their frustration. They feel lost, alone, and scared with having to go through the process. Fourteen years of phone calls, text messages, and emails and they're never "Hey Nick, how are you doing?" It's wave after wave of scared children who are afraid that they're going to go to jail like a bad guy. They lash out and find the person closest to them in the process to take out their frustration on, me. I should have been a dentist, you make bank and you get all the free teeth you want.

Some stereotypes are true and there's a lot of shitty criminal defense lawyers out there. There are also ones that do a good job for their clients as well. Honestly, I'm not sure where I fit in on that wide spectrum, because I have what my therapist calls a "strong negativity bias." NO, I DON'T, LAURA!!! I allow my client's situation to affect me. Client's have told me that I'm different than other lawyers because I care about what happens. If caring about your clients problems makes me afraid, irritated, and angry, then I'd rather not care so much. I don't have proper boundaries to have this job. I have all of the feels but don't have the thick skin to deal with it. Instead of dealing with my clients' problems at arms length, I let them get close to me and affect me. If they go to jail, I feel like I'm going to jail.

Enough feelings-talk for a minute, back to the alleged murderer. Which reminds me, I think if you're on trial for murder and you threaten to kill your lawyer, then I don't have to refer to you as "alleged murderer" anymore. If you threaten to kill the only person that's trying to help you, there's a good chance you I did it. With that off my chest, let's continue.

The law says that the prosecutor has the burden of proof and I don't have to prepare a defense but I thought it would be a good idea to have something to say during this murder trial. I'd like to avoid a huge embarrassing failure. I could just picture it: The judge would be like "Mr. Leydorf, do you have an opening statement?" Then everyone in the courtroom would turn to me as I pick rotisserie chicken out of that space between my molars and say "Nah, I'm good." The fear of embarrassment is a great motivator for me so I decided that I needed to get very prepared for this case. I spent countless hours getting ready. I can tell you that it wasn't the money that was a motivator for me in this case. I was getting paid $60 an hour to try and keep another man from going to prison for the rest of his life. (they've now raised the rates across Michigan to $100.00, which is better, I guess but it's still not enough to put up with some asshole threatening to kill you)

56

I reviewed police reports. Leave it to a police officer to make a murder boring. Words like assailant and perpetrator are overused and unnecessary. Just say what you're trying to say. "The dude that killed the other dude shot him with this gun that we found in the shitter." Sure, it's not very precise but at least it's interesting to read! I looked at too many pictures of a dead person. It all made me sad. The guy that died seemed like a good guy. In the interviews that the police did with his family members they said that he'd do anything for anyone. All he did was sell weed. Was it a crime at the time? Yes. Did he deserve to have his house broken into and shot while his little girl was in the other room? No. That girl's life changed forever that night.

In the midst of pouring over all of these videos, and photos, and reports, there's a feeling that starts to come over me. I'd felt it in other cases, but this time it was stronger. It wasn't a loud and angry emotion, it was a fog. It was transparent, but visible to me. It demanded my attention after I read one more witness statement. The fog, I mean it wasn't an actual fog, I'm not crazy. I'm a lawyer, but I'm not crazy, I swear. The fog was saying "even if you win, you lose." The fog was right. This man was dead. If I "win" in the traditional "My Cousin Vinny" sense, there's a man that's still dead and a baby that's going to grow up without a father.

Law in the Times of Corona

As I'm writing this[1], we are in the middle of a global pandemic. What's scary to me is that there are some people who don't agree with that last sentence. The global pandemic part. I think we all can agree that things are totally different than before we knew what COVID-19 was. One thing that has changed dramatically is the practice of law. I love that things are different and I hope the new normal for the practice of law is here to stay, because the law has been straight up dumb ever since I started practicing in 2006. It makes me sound old to read that.

The biggest change has been that we can conduct hearings online. We've had videoconferencing for years but it took a global pandemic for the law to implement it on a day to day basis. There's no reason why these changes shouldn't have been made across the profession years ago. It's hard to calculate how much of my time was wasted per week on court. I'd have to get up early, drive to my office, put on a suit, grab my files, drive to court and then wait. I'm not talking about the waiting that you'd do in line at a Subway for your turkey bacon ranch while the old lady ahead of you is oversharing with the Sandwich Artist that green pepper makes her

---

[1] Yes, it took me forever to finish this book. STOP JUDGING ME!!!

gassy kind of waiting. I'm talking about waiting of biblical proportions. The kind of waiting where you forget why the fuck you're even where you are kind of waiting. The kind of waiting that makes you question your own existence kind of waiting.

The problem is judges. Sorry judges who are reading this. If you're a judge and you made it this far, you know I'm right. Judges have complete control over their calendar. They're the king or queen of their little fiefdom. They are the ones that choose to schedule 98 motherfucking hearings all at 9:00am on a Monday morning. It makes no goddamn sense. When I explain this to non-lawyers they look at me like I'm making this up. I'm not. It happens every goddamn day in courtrooms all across this country. It doesn't matter if the hearing is going to take 2 minutes or 30 minutes, they're scheduled all at the same time.

When I discovered this, it definitely was a shock to my system. I remember when I first started out being a lawyer. I took assigned cases for people who couldn't afford lawyers. I had one case at city hall in downtown Lansing. I was prepared to the max. I got there early. I paid for parking. I got in the elevator and got off on the 6th floor to discover an absolute shit show. The only way I can describe is like triage but for law. People were standing around, there weren't any open seats left to sit. Babies were crying. Hell, I saw a lawyer ready to cry too. It was a mess.

I found the courtroom that I needed and it was empty. I knew I needed to find the prosecutor, so I looked for him. I found him in a room with 4 police officers trying to get their overtime slips approved. I waited. And I waited. I waited for a half an hour and it was finally my turn. I spoke with the prosecutor and by spoke I mean I didn't get a word in before he recited the bullshit plea offer that his boss had made for my client. My client had more felonies than I could count so my client's thinking was "what's one more, Nick?!"

I leave the room and find my client to share with him what this "offer" was from the prosecutor. He tells me to tell the prosecutor to go fuck himself. I tell my client "I'll pass that along." So now we're going to have to run a preliminary hearing on a case where my guy allegedly eluded the police in his car and when they finally got him, he fought with them. Oh, the best part is that he threw drugs before he ran from the police. Sorry, I lied. The best part of it all was it was all on video. The only question for the judge at this preliminary hearing was whether there was probable cause to believe that a crime was committed and probable cause to believe my client committed a crime. Did my client probably commit a crime? You bet your sweet ass he did. Was there a reason to hold this hearing? Absolutely not. Was I going to have to do it anyway? Yup!

I go and find the prosecutor to talk with him again. Maybe if I turn on the ol' Leydorf charm I can talk my client into some kind of plea offer. Something would have been better than nothing. I made a point to not lead with "Hey, my client says you can go fuck yourself, bud." The prosecutor said what prosecutors say when they want to dig their heels, "the offer is the offer." Thanks, dickhead for the existential hot take. Well kids, it looks like I'm going to be running my first ever preliminary hearing this morning.

I let the clerk know what's going on. She barely acknowledges my presence. She doesn't look up from her computer and tells me "I'll put your file in the stack." Stack doesn't sound good. The term stack sounds almost like a pile, and piles are not good either. I waited for some kind of human response, a look or gesture but got nothing. I knew it was going to be awhile.

I plopped myself down on the wooden bench in the back of the courtroom. The benches were long, like comedically long. It looked like they got them from a church. They were like 20 feet long and every time someone in had to get up to leave, it meant that everyone had to get up and leave. Just one of the inefficiencies. Nothing happened in the courtroom for 15 minutes. I decided to get up and walk around. My client sees me and asks how long it's going to be. Oh, you have someplace to be? For this guy, the wait wasn't so bad because it would ensure that he'd remain crime-free for the time being.

I walked around and saw a sheet with the court docket. I saw the time, 8:30am. There were 17 cases scheduled for 8:30am. The problem was that mine was scheduled for 9:30am. Another problem was that there were 14 scheduled for 9:30am. It was now 10:03am and it didn't look like anything was going to start happening anytime soon. Please send help.

Back to judges. They have the power to keep this kind of shit from happening. If you are able to make people stand up when you enter a room, then you have the ability to not schedule 14 cases for the same time. It's like they get derive some form of pleasure from creating a colossal clusterfuck of bullshit by scheduling so many things at the same time. The ability to sense inefficiencies of a system is coded into my DNA from my German ancestry. It makes my eye twitch just thinking about it. If you were wondering, it's the left one.

"How can you schedule all of those things at different times, Nick?" Excellent question, judge, I mean your honor. You stagger them. If there are 14 things, you set no more than 2 at the same time at 15 minute intervals. Then that saves everyone time from having to rush around to be there for a hearing that's not going to happen two hours after you were supposed to be there. It also means that police officers aren't getting paid overtime on their day off to sit around and talk cop shit with the other cops waiting for their hearing to happen.

Back to me and this preliminary hearing. I learn that I'm third in line for hearings that were actually going to happen. The first one is a domestic violence situation and they're waiting for the wife of the defendant to show so they can proceed. She doesn't. Case dismissed. Justice dispensed. Kinda. One down, one more to go.

The second case was a possession of cocaine. The fight was about the traffic stop. The younger defense lawyer was trying to set up a motion to dismiss in the higher court but it wasn't working too well. The cop on the stand had been down this road before and was deploying the proverbial spike strips on the path toward dismissal. It seemed like the cop answered every question with "in my training and experience." Ugh, just talk like a human being, dude. There's nothing more annoying than a cop on the stand saying things like "perpetrator" or "then I proceeded to." No one talks like that. When you've been waiting for over an hour and a half for your hearing to start, that kind of shit annoys you. I could feel my eyes roll back in my head every time that smug police officer opened his mouth. Oh, it's now 11:30am.

After the 37th question phrased just a bit differently than the last, the defense attorney said he had no other questions. The judge ruled from the bench that there was probable cause and the case was going to be sent to the higher court for the next hearings. Hallelujah, my case was up.

The judge stands and says "we'll be back at 1pm to continue the morning's docket." I'm like what the fuck? I was livid and I stand up and say "your honor, I'm the last case for the morning's docket and I've been here since 8:30." She rolls her eyes and walks off the bench. She's now in the Court of Appeals.

I came back at 1pm. The hearing lasted all of 9 minutes. My client spent the next 15 telling me how the cop lied on the stand. The problem was that there was video and unless there was some grand conspiracy at work to get my dumbass client, the video shows my client throwing a baggie with white powder in it while he's running from the police. My client asks me "what do you think we should do?" I wanted to say, "stop committing crimes," but I said "I'll continue to talk with them and see if we can get a better offer."

Things are completely different now. It's sad that it took a pandemic for things to change. When the Michigan governor issued the shelter in place order was going to take effect, I went to my office and brought my computer and my files at home. I had no idea what was going to happen. "Was I going to have to go to court? How was I going to meet with clients?" It was scary because while there was a pandemic going on, there was a pandemic that I'd been suffering with for years, debt. Student loans to be precise. Those bastards weren't going to go away and I needed to pay the bills.

It turns out that a good old fashioned pandemic was just what I needed to get my ass in gear. I was able to automate my new client intake process. Previously, I had a system where I would mail my clients a packet of information so that they could review it and be prepared for our meeting. I thought that maybe I shouldn't be sending things through the mail when we were all freaking out about whether we were going to get COVID-19. I had to figure out how to automate that by myself.

I had never done a client meeting via Zoom before. It wasn't something that I had even thought of. The traditional lawyer model had always been, if you want to meet with me you have to come to my brick and mortar office. Well, that just wasn't possible anymore.

I could have done two things and each one of them would have been acceptable: first, cry in my basement and wait for someone to save me (I did that for a day or so) or second, I could figure out a way to do things differently. That's who I am anyway. I don't like doing things that I'm supposed to do. I like to do shit like wear two different colored socks (I'm doing that now) or start doing stand-up comedy at 32 years old with a two-month old baby at home.

A couple of weeks went by and I could feel an energetic shift. At the beginning of the shelter in place order, I was suffering from tremendous headaches. It felt like I was dizzy and in the morning I could hardly stand. It was weird. My wife, who is into woo-woo shit, said that it was because everything that we had been doing suddenly stopped. I read somewhere that there was a noticeable decrease in the earth's seismic activity because people weren't going anywhere. That's wild.

I enjoyed the time that I was working exclusively from home. I blocked out my calendar. I would divide my day up into chunks of time. For an hour in the morning, I would write. For another hour, I would block off exercise. Just like pre-quarantine, I didn't do that either, but hey it was nice to at least block it off.

I also dedicated time during the day for self-care. In the mornings, I would go over a list I had made of the things I was grateful for. I even found an app that I had downloaded on my phone that allows you to record you saying affirmations and it plays them back for you. 20 year old Nick would have said that this was definitely some weird woo-woo bullshit but that Nick wasn't as cool as the 39 year old version of me.

As the days went on, I felt like I was doing things different and that energized me. One week I had my biggest week ever in terms of business. It felt amazing. For the first time ever, I was enjoying being a lawyer and I have to say that there was quite a thrill with not having to go to court anymore.

Courts started new ways of conducting hearings over Zoom. This was something that they weren't familiar with and something that I'd never done before. It was amazing. I can tell you that there's no greater thrill than defending another man's life and doing it while you're in your basement not wearing pants. Law in the times of COVID meant that you only have to look like a lawyer from the waist up. If you're putting on dress pants to do a Zoom hearing, you're doing it wrong.

I can honestly say that during COVID I have also seen some of the wildest shit happen during a court hearing. One morning I logged in to the court's Zoom hearing room and there were 4 other people there - a judge, a prosecutor, a defense lawyer, and a defendant. What was remarkable about the defendant was that he was wearing sunglasses and no shirt. I had to mute myself and take myself off video because I didn't want to laugh during the middle of what seemed like a tense moment. I don't know much about that case but I can tell you this - that guy was not guilty. Only innocent people have the balls to show up for a hearing where they could go to jail with sunglasses and no shirt.

Another morning, I showed up for a hearing, and there was a judge and two defense lawyers in the Zoom meeting room. One female defense lawyer spent 10 minutes fixing her hair while we were discussing what was going to happen. Two things about that. First, I'm jealous because I'm bald and I haven't had to fix my hair since the first George Bush was president. Second, a Zoom court hearing isn't your mirror. Take 5 minutes, fix your hair, and be done with it.

Another Zoom court fail I want to share with you was pretty hilarious and sad. I log in to the court's Zoom hearing room, and I see that there's a judge with his face too close to the camera. I wanted to type something in the chat box like "hey judge, I wanna object that you haven't trimmed your nose hairs, dude!" But I thought that wasn't a good idea. In addition to the judge, there was a defense lawyer and a woman, who was the defendant. This appeared to be a sentencing hearing. You could tell that the defense lawyer had not talked to his client ahead of time, or if he did, he was doing it wrong. The defendant was holding her phone in her hand, and it was moving around like she was in an earthquake. I was getting nauseous just from watching her. Also, and most notably, she was smoking. By that I mean she wasn't on fire. No, she was smoking a cigarette. Smoking. During a sentencing hearing. I said to myself, "What the fuck is happening, dawg?" It was wild. I think it's a safe rule to have that if it's something that you can't do while you're physically in court, it's something that you shouldn't be doing while you're in Zoom Court. For instance, you shouldn't be doing the dishes, or beating your kids, or taking a shit. And even if you're a disinterested French person, you absolutely should not be smoking during your sentencing hearing. There is an unless to that, unless immediately after your sentencing, you're going to be shot by firing squad, then I'll let it pass.

The absolute best so far was a hearing when I was least expecting something crazy to happen. Life has a way of throwing these enjoyable moments to keep things interesting. I logged in early for my hearing, and I see that there's one taking place already. There's a judge and a person in a t-shirt driving a car. At first, I didn't recognize the person because they were wearing a t-shirt and driving their car. When they looked at the camera, I was able to recognize the guy because this person is a defense attorney whom I see around when I go to court. So let me paint this picture for you - a defense attorney shows up for Zoom Court in a V-neck t-shirt while driving his car and thinks that this is acceptable. This time, the spirit so moved me that I said, "Come on," during the hearing before muting myself. What kind of fucking idiot would think that would be okay? I could see if it was a normal person, and they were dropped on their head and had no concept of what you're supposed to do in court. But this dude is a fucking lawyer. Not a good one, obviously, but he's a lawyer! In full disclosure, I wasn't wearing pants, but at least the judge couldn't see that! Come on, fam! We gotta step our games up.

I fault these judges for not saying something. The only person who said something was the judge presiding over the hearing with the smoking lady. When the judge said they were going to take a recess because she and her lawyer clearly had not spoken and there was no way they could do the hearing, he did say, "When we come back on the record, I want you to refrain from smoking, ma'am." That's the best Zoom quote I've heard thus far. Times are different for law and as long as I don't have to go to court, I'm loving every minute of it.

How the Sausage is Made

In college, people would ask me about becoming a lawyer, and they'd ask, "How could you defend someone you know did it?" I was 20 years old, trying to take over the world one Natty Light at a time, so I had my prepared answer that included trite phrases like "for the system to work, both sides have to do their job," or "it's the prosecutor's job to prove that a defendant is guilty, that's not for me to decide." Those all may be true. But here's the thing, they don't make me feel good inside when I say them. It doesn't instill inside of me a feeling of honor by having to do mental gymnastics to create a justification so I can sit with my family and enjoy a movie on our couch together on Friday nights.

I kept going, even as the fog surrounded me. While the human part of me struggled with what it meant to defend someone charged with murder, another part of me felt that if I were to win, it would be my masterpiece. People would say, "Did you hear Leydorf won that murder trial? Leydorf, isn't he that handsome, bald lawyer? Let's get matching tattoos of his face on our upper arms in his honor!!!" It would be the kind of win that Matt Damon had in "The Rainmaker." No one expected him to win, but he worked hard and really pulled that one out of his ass. Accordingly, it deserved some well-earned time to fuck off for a minute.

However, Matt Damon's character, Rudy Baylor, won a third of fifty million dollars, which back in 1997 was some real "fuck you" money. By comparison, I was on track to make $47 dollars at the end of this trial.

Work was affecting my sleep. I'd be at the office all the time. On top of it, I'd have other cases too. I'd be reviewing transcripts of the preliminary hearing for the murder case, and my phone would bing-bong at me that I had to be in court. It was humbling to go from preparing for a murder trial, one of the most difficult things a lawyer can ever do, to go to court to deal with a speeding ticket. Luckily, I'd catch myself before I'd say the things I'd wanted to say, like "Listen, Brad, the officer got you with a fucking radar gun at 17 over the speed limit and only wrote you for 5 over. Just pay the ticket so we can get the fuck outta here? BUT WHAT ABOUT THE POINTS ON MY LICENSE, NICK?!" I'd swallow my pride and go in the back and beg with the prosecutor, giving my famous tap dancing number in the key of C, "He's a Good Guy!" and they'd reduce it to something that the evil insurance companies wouldn't be able to use to jack up his insurance. Brad was grateful to hear the news, and he assured me he'll pay me next week.

Which makes me think, every lawyer says that their client is a "good guy." (I'm using the pronoun guy here because women rarely do stupid shit, I didn't leave you out of this on purpose, ladies) I guess it's because no lawyer, no matter how unscrupulous, is going to put on a suit, walk into a room with the prosecutor and say, "Listen, my client is a huge bag of shit, can you just give me a deal anyway?"

Back to sleep. It was noteworthy because I wasn't getting any of it. When I was, it was filled with weird dreams. I'd go to court with no pants on, which I can confirm I have never done. (who knew that in 2020 I'd routinely appear for court on Zoom without pants?) Or the one where the judge had the head of a dragon and the body of a judge, and when I said something, the dragon/judge chimera breathed fire on my briefcase and set it on fire. Those were the fun ones. A lot of nights, it was just me dreaming about driving to court, and I'd be mumbling to myself, going over evidence. Many nights, my wife would wake me up and tell me that I yelled "objection" in my sleep. It was frustrating because she'd never tell me if the dragon judge sustained or overruled my objection.

Through the fevered dreams of pantsless trips to court and dragon judges incinerating my work product, I was able to get somewhere and prepare some decent building blocks of a defense. Like my JV baseball coach said, "You can't make chicken salad out of chicken shit." He was a real wordsmith. But he's right. I was doing the best I could do with a case where 4 out of 5 co-defendants said my client shot this guy. 4 out of 5 criminals also recommend taking a plea deal when you're facing life in prison without the possibility of parole. But my client was a non-conformist. When everyone zigged, he zagged. When everyone wasn't murdering, he, well... When everyone took a plea, he wanted to have his trial. He wanted to be the star of the show. Well, the stage was being set, the lights were on, and the trial was waiting for us. By us, I mean me, because all he had to do was fucking sit there and shut the fuck up.

Free Consultation

If you've ever seen a lawyer ad before, then "free consultation" is a phrase that you're familiar with. After 18 years of being a lawyer, I can safely say that free consultation is the dumbest fucking thing that a lawyer has ever come up with. However, it's something that every lawyer feels compelled to do. Charge for my time to meet with me? I don't know.

A free consultation makes no sense to me. Setting aside whether it was a good decision or not, I went to school to be a lawyer. I did 4 years of undergrad and 3 years of law school. When I graduated, I accumulated 6 figures in student loan debt. My student loan debt is bigger than the gross domestic product of some third-world countries. Despite all that, I have to offer a free consultation and give my time away to some asshole on the phone because a shitty lawyer 50 years ago who couldn't get any clients came up with the idea of giving away their time for free. It's stupid. I will say, however, that offering a free consultation has been one of the ways that I have been able to generate some comedy gold.

During the 18 years of being a lawyer, I have always offered a free consultation. Upon reflection, it's weird to me that I blindly followed that outdated model of offering it because I typically just say fuck you to the things that everyone else does. I think it's because I have an Aquarius rising sign or whatever. This is one of those things that I'm uncovering by writing this book that may make me look at how I do things and do them differently from now on.

The person who took home the award for the craziest person that I've talked to during a phone consultation was the guy who wanted to sue the government because they stole his baby. I know, right? It already sounds like a good call. It has all the pieces of a compelling story: a guy, the government, and a baby. Strap in, because this one gets bumpy quick.

For years, I would answer my own phone. At first, I wore it as a badge of honor because I thought that gave me a personal connection with anyone who called my office. If you wanted me, you got me. Sometimes it would surprise people. I'd answer the phone and I'd tell them it's me, and they're like, "What the hell, you're the guy I tried to call? What kind of scam is this?!" Years later, I would come to my senses because I learned the hard way why no one does this. You have to have someone answer your phone because the more successful you become, the more you're going to have to deal with crazy people. That said, this happened during the period in my career where I thought I could be all things to all people. The reality was that I was spending hours on the phone with people who had legal problems but wanted shit for free - read "they have no money."

The crazy people's stories always happen unexpectedly. This guy, let's just call him Dwayne (that's not his name, but I think it's a tad more useful to give him a name rather than call him guy), calls me out of the blue right as I'm getting ready to leave for court. The phone rings, and I answer it while I'm doing 13 things to be able to walk out the door. I am the kind of person who forgets 12 of those things, and I have to walk back into the office to get what I forgot, so I don't know why I answered the phone call, probably because I have an incessant need to be liked. I could have let it go to voicemail, but the universe and my ego thought that Dwayne and I should speak.

I answer the call and put the phone between my head and right shoulder (my right ear is my phone ear - I don't know what phone ear you guys are, but that's my go-to) as I'm walking around my office. Without exchanging pleasantries, Dwayne gets right in there and starts talking. No foreplay, he wants to get right to it. In a way, I respect that because I'm not getting paid for this, so I have no interest in the typical "how's the weather?" small talk. Dwayne is already knee deep in this story, and he's already left me back at the shore. He's on the third paragraph of the manuscript, and I am still reading the acknowledgments and cover page, trying to figure out who wrote this book.

I stop Dwayne and ask him for his name. He stops and is out of the gate, annoyed with me because I messed with his flow by trying to figure out who the fuck I'm talking with. He tells me his name, and he says, "Mr. Leydorf, I need your help. (dramatic pause) The Government (pause) stole my baby." There should have been some dramatic music playing that a producer would have dropped at that point in the call for effect.

I repeat back the last sentence to Dwayne as I'm putting my suit pants on, "The Government stole your baby?" I've found that when people spew some whackadoo shit, I typically repeat it back to them in order to avoid laughing in their faces. Crazy people really don't like that, even though I think, at some level, the universe throws crazy people into our lives for comedic effect.

While I don't have time for this call, now I'm intrigued. I tell Dwayne that I'm in a hurry to get to court and that I'd love to talk with him about this government baby-stealing conspiracy theory, but the same government that stole his baby is going to hold me in contempt if I don't make it to this court hearing on time. I waited for a laugh because that was a solid off-the-cuff joke, but Dwayne was having nothing of it. Dwayne was all business. I guess he was still salty from the government stealing his baby and all.

Dwayne retorts with "Mr. Leydorf, I need to speak with you urgently about this. I was referred to you by Regina Johnson (that's not her name). She said you helped her with her case and that you would be the man that would be able to help me." A couple of things with that. I never had a client named Regina Johnson and if I did, I would call her immediately and cuss her out for sending ol' Dwayne my way. I have a strict "don't refer people to me that are nuttier than squirrel turds" policy.

I'm like, "Dwayne, I want to listen to what you have to say, but I have to go." Dwayne isn't having any of it. He's like "real quick, real quick, Mr. Leydorf." Having heard that, one would be safe to assume that what could come out of ol' Dwayne's suck hole would be a relatively brief story, and we'd make plans to connect, and before then, I would change my number. But not ol' Dwayne. Crazy people are persistent, especially when someone isn't charging them for their time.

I say, "Ok, Dwayne, real quick." Dwayne says, "Ok, I'll make this real quick. 18 years ago, the government came and stole my baby." Dammit, Dwayne, this isn't going to be real quick. I need the elevator version of this story, and you're giving me the eight-part Netflix documentary version. I need to be on the road right now, not being sucked into the shit vacuum that is your life. Yes, I know I could have just ended the call, but remember what I said about my need to be liked? If I hung up on Dwayne, he wouldn't like me. If Dwayne didn't like me, my ego tells me that there's a high probability that I'd die.

Having said that, I am genuinely interested in this story. I had many follow-up questions for Dwayne. First off, why would the government want a baby, let alone your baby? The government doesn't have time to take care of a baby! (cue the "ain't nobody got time for that!" GIF). What makes your baby so special? Dwayne seemed like a no-nonsense kind of guy, so I held back that very pressing line of questioning.

Also, the government stole your baby 18 years ago. Math was never really my strong suit, but this isn't a baby anymore. 18 years ago it was. Now it's not. From the brief time I had known Dwayne, I felt safe to ask at least a preliminary query about why it's taken so long to do something to report this baby stolen. As I'm straightening my tie and looking at myself in the reflection of my diploma, I ask Dwayne why it took so long to call someone about this? There's a brief pause, and Dwayne retorts, "I got busy." I paused, rolled my eyes into the back of my head, and made preparations to end this call immediately. Jesus Christ, Dwayne, I gotta say I'm taking the government's side on this one. 18 years, fam?!

I could relate to Dwayne because I'm a parent too, and I know how busy one can get to be an adult. I can safely say that if the government stole my baby, I'd be pretty miffed about it, too. After the government left with the baby, however, is when I'd get on the horn to complain about it. I know that we all have busy lives, so I'll give Dwayne the benefit of the doubt. Let's say that your favorite Seinfeld episode was coming on right after this theft takes place, and you don't wanna miss the one with Kramer and the Kenny Rogers chicken. What do you do? You put it on your to-do list for tomorrow. You write, "Tomorrow - get to the bottom of why the government stole my baby." I guess some other things came up for Dwayne over the next 18 years, and this random Friday afternoon at 12:42 pm was the time that his schedule cleared and he had the time necessary to address it.

Here's my take on the idea of a free consultation. It comes across as desperate. Let's compare other professions where people are compensated for their time. Hookers are a good example. While I've never patronized a hooker, I can assume that if you came to them with a problem (not came on them - hey-o!) and said "listen, ma'am, I am in dire need of your services" I would gather from my working knowledge of hookers based on my studies of them from afar like Sir David Attenborough that they wouldn't be like "oh honey, no problem, I'll suck yo' dick for free!" But that's exactly what a free consultation is. You're fixing people's problems and getting nothing for it. Other than a funny story that I got to tell in this book you're reading, I didn't get anything from Dwayne. Yeah, there wasn't some big payday once we figured out who stole this kid 18 years ago; the missing piece of the puzzle was more than likely that Dwayne was off his meds. There was no instant payoff either. I was late for court, but it wasn't like I could tell the judge, "Hey, Your Honor, sorry I'm late. I got sucked into a time warp talking with this crazy asshole Dwayne!" and the judge was like, "You mean the guy who had his baby stolen by the government? How's he doing?!"

The notion of a free consultation is nothing more than a beacon that attracts crazy people. In the crashing waves that are people's problems, a free consultation is a lighthouse that they see where they can enjoy a respite from the storm. Everyone has a story. Crazy people have lots of them, and some of them are true. They've shared those crazy stories with their families to the point where their families make up an excuse every time they try and tell it. I'm sure every time ol' Dwayne starts to tell that baby-stealing story to his sister, she makes an excuse to get herself out of the room. "I'm sorry, Dwayne, I ate some bad Indian food last night, and I have to shit like you wouldn't believe."

However, I understand the idea of a free consultation. It's a marketing tool to get people to talk with you, and then if they feel comfortable with you, then they'll hire you. Unfortunately, crazy people really ruin the return on investment. Nothing against crazy people, but in my experience, I've only had the privilege of having free consultations with people that are bat shit crazy AND have zero money. Maybe someday I'll be able to snag a rich old eccentric gentleman with a shit load of problems and a 7-figure trust fund, but until that day comes, I'll have someone answer my phone for me.

Pre-Trial Shitters

The night before the trial, I knew that I wasn't going to be able to sleep. I decided to try and just go into our bedroom and lie there and pray for the sleep fairy to douche me with fairy dust. I hadn't gone to bed at 8 pm before that. I felt like a super old person who just finished up watching Jeopardy and Wheel of Fortune back to back, complained that Vanna's dress was too suggestive, and was ready to call it a day.

I don't remember much of what I dreamed that night, but I do remember that my wife didn't wake me up, saying I tried to kill her in my sleep or anything like that. I remember that I was up at 5 am, and I felt like shit. I couldn't get my body out of the fight-or-flight mode it was in. There were days leading up to the first day of trial that I actually considered for more than 8 minutes just running away. Not literally running away, I was struggling with gout. I was stress-eating so much garbage. I was like a rest area raccoon, and my gout was flaring like a mother fucker, so I mean figuratively running away. But it's hard to run away when you have a wife and a kid, because they'll probably find you. And I guess I love them, or whatever. It's times like that where I think of that movie "Into the Wild" with that guy who lives in a van in Alaska, and he dies there alone. It makes me cry thinking about it. I'm crying about it now as I'm writing this. This trial evoked a range of emotions in me. Emotions that I still haven't dealt with. To the point that I considered leaving my life behind to escape it. Leaving my office and never going back. I fantasized about taking my work cell phone and smashing the shit out of it with the Louisville Slugger bat my dad got me when I was 8 years old, with Wade Boggs's autograph burnt into it.

But I didn't run away. I got up, made the coffee, and showered that morning. I did the thing I do when I'm under so much stress that I put items away in their wrong places. In law school, I'd be under so much stress that I'd put the milk in the cupboard and the cereal in the refrigerator. The morning of the first day of the trial, I turned the coffee pot on, I put the grounds in there, and poured the water, but didn't turn it on because I was thinking about my opening statement. I was so awake I didn't need coffee. I've heard clients tell me that meth is amazing because it makes you feel like everything in your brain is turned on. Well, they should try handling a murder trial. It's safer, and you don't have to worry about losing your teeth.

I was up, and I had to do something because it was too early to go to court. If I went to court that early, the courthouse would have been closed, and it would have looked like I was one of those assholes waiting in line for the new iPhone. So I went to my office for some last-minute prep. I do this out of habit when I get stressed before big events. I'll go to my office to, I guess, try and convince myself that I'm putting every last possible minute into a big project. At the time, I felt that if I was defending someone's life, I shouldn't have a life of my own. This was my first murder trial on my own, so I wanted to be prepared. In those moments when I'm preparing, I'm not getting anything accomplished. It's like my brain is just saying "fuck, fuck, fuck" and my arms are just moving papers around. My body has a unique reaction to stress, which makes getting work done during stressful times particularly challenging. I've read about "fight or flight mode" that your body goes into. It's a pretty cool idea that we needed when humans were living in caves. Our brain tells the rest of our body to wake the fuck up and pay attention because something is about to go down. "Hey, there's a lion over there! Oh shit, everyone on high alert!" Humans still experience this now, even though there aren't many lions out here trying to kill us. The only way a lion is going to kill me as I write this is if it escaped from the zoo, took an Uber, and broke into my office. If a lion did that, I wouldn't even be mad that it killed me; I'd appreciate the effort.

My body goes to an extra level when it's confronted with stress. I get the typical narrowed vision and rapid heartbeat, and flushed face. However, my body decides to kick in a little bonus: my ass sweats, and I have to shit a lot. I'm glad I live in a time now where there are no active predators because I would definitely die if I were a caveman with these symptoms when I got scared. There's no way I'm able to get away from a lion when I have to stop to shit every 4 seconds. Maybe my prolific shitting would have actually been a next-level defense mechanism because no lion is going to want to eat prey with a sweaty ass and that's covered in their own shit. The lion would probably let me live. I'd have a great story to tell my cavewoman wife that night when I came home crying, covered in my own excrement.

After I put in a sufficient amount of non-preparing preparation, I climbed into my Nissan Altima (I'm just being factual here, I'm not bragging) and backed out of the driveway in my office, scraping the curb like I do all the time, and started driving to the courthouse. I do that Every. Goddamn. Time.

Law School in Miami

The summer after I graduated from Michigan State was a busy one. I had narrowed down my choices of law schools to two: Michigan State and the University of Miami, not the one in Ohio, the one in Florida.

At the time, I thought they were both great schools. On one hand, I could stay in Michigan and live through hellish winter after hellish winter, or I could live in Miami, where it never snows. Sorry, MSU, I'm getting the fuck out of East Lansing.

A few weeks before I made my decision, I went down to Miami with my mom and dad to check the place out. The only time that I had been to Florida before that was when I was in the high school marching band. We took a 30-hour bus trip down to Florida and marched in a parade at Disney World. Sure, it technically was a band tour bus, but there weren't any groupies or coke.

The trip was so long that I went nuts and flipped out. I should have flown down there and met the other nerds, marched with Mickey, done a couple of bumps with some Cubans in South Beach, and flown home. No human should be on a bus for that long. It was like some kind of psychological experiment to determine who was going to break first. It was me. It broke my brain.

The car ride down to Miami with my parents wasn't as bad, but I made a deal with myself that if the trip is anything over 20 hours again, let's splash the cash and take a goddamn plane, or I'm going to end up freaking out and taking my pants off in a Denny's in Alabama. I mean, it's Alabama, that kind of shit might go unnoticed, but it's a good plan nonetheless.

There was one person whom I knew in Miami, who was a friend of my parents. He was also a Michigan ex-pat who migrated down to Florida to live there full-time. Not some snowbird bullshit either. He pulled up stakes and moved down there. I had never met him before, but my mom said he was a private investigator. That sounded badass. Me going to law school and working with a PI? I would be riding in a Ferrari Testarossa, driving a jet boat in no time. Cue the Miami Vice theme song. My only concern was that I had an overly sensitive nose, so I'd had to adjust to all the cocaine. That's three cocaine references in four paragraphs if you're playing at home.

I knew nothing of Miami, and that blissful ignorance helped seal the deal for me to move there. The 1,439 miles from Bannister to Coral Gables was enough of a selling point. The visit to Miami was a perfunctory gesture; I had my mind made up, and even if I was robbed at gunpoint and forced to be a drug mule, I was willing to give the city as a whole a free pass.

When we met Jeff, the PI, he showed us around the city. I wasn't really paying too much attention; I was trying to deal with the anxiety of what living in a big city would mean. Luckily, I didn't find Miami to be that at all. The University of Miami is in Coral Gables, which is a part of the city. I was so busy during my year of law school there, I can't tell you whether it is north or south of Miami, but it's somewhere close. It's somewhere down in the tip of the penis that is Florida. In 2002, Coral Gables was pretty quiet. To be honest, I haven't been back since and don't plan to either. Foreshadowing.

Like the decision to go to law school in the first place, the decision to move to Miami wasn't well thought out either. I'm sure you're discovering a pattern here. Looking back, it seems that the years 1998-2005 were a sleepwalk for me. I can't tell you what I did or why I did what I did. Despite all the drug references in this book, I wasn't doing that many drugs. I was a fully functioning adult, at least on the outside. As I would later discover, I had never dealt with situations that needed to be dealt with on an emotional level. I took the attitude of "I'll get to it later" and just never did. That's not the way to move throughout your life. Don't procrastinate with big emotions, bud. You're going to end up paying for it later. It's like a credit card but with a much higher rate of interest, and ultimately, the stakes are higher if you don't pay. If you don't pay your credit card bill, your credit score is going to suffer, and you won't be able to move into that apartment you want. If you don't deal with your emotions, over time the interest is going to accrue, and you'll have a panic attack in a Publix Grocery store in Coral Gables, Florida. If that happens, go to the frozen food section. The cold helps you get your shit together.

While I should have taken a year after college to get a fucking grip on who I was and what I wanted to become, I didn't. I decided to power through. Why wait a year? I would be doing the same thing in a year anyway, right? I felt the pressure of being left behind. I didn't know what FOMO (fear of missing out) was at the time, but looking back and comparing how I felt, it sure seems like the same thing. I needed to pick a career before I got too old, so I could do amazing things before I turned 30 years old. The problem was, I wasn't emotionally ready to pick a career. Unfortunately, I had already committed to going to law school, and I felt like there was no turning back. There was, but I didn't believe that was an option.

My incessant drive to achieve and succeed was yelling louder than the part of my brain that wanted me to relax and take it easy.

I didn't get any scholarships from any schools to go to law school. Nothing. I worked my ass off during college to get the best grades that I could, and it amounted to absolute bupkis. To be fair, I don't know if that is fair to blame not getting scholarships on anyone other than myself. I didn't do the work necessary to look for schools that would help pay my law school tuition. I had heard that Cooley Law School in Lansing would give people scholarships. However, I also researched them, and they would take absolutely anyone and everyone. It was more difficult to get struck by lightning than it was to get into Cooley Law School. They also produced Trump's doofus-stooge Michael Cohen, so looking back on it, not going to Cooley was one good decision that I made during that time.

I relied on my grades and work, and test scores alone to get me into a good law school. You know, the things that should matter. What a rube. Shockingly, it didn't happen. I applied to a lot of schools and only got into three - Michigan State, Penn State, and the University of Miami. Looking back, I'm concerned why I was so appealing to universities that have a documented penchant for scandal. I didn't know at the time that every one of them was going to shit the bed publicly, so I picked the only one that had gone through public disgrace at the time, The U.

Not getting a scholarship meant that I would have to use student loans to pay my tuition and living expenses. If you're reading this and are considering going to law school, or any school for that matter, you need to seriously consider what you're doing when you sign that paperwork. Things are a bit different now because there's been a national conversation that has been ongoing for years about student loans. However, back in 2002, things were much different. We hadn't gone through the first of many economic collapses that would be on the way. Back in 2002, if you were to become a lawyer, you weren't going to have to worry about money. Being a lawyer would mean that your quality of life would drastically improve, and the level of income that you would be receiving would far surpass any concerns about the 6 figures in debt that you would be about to take on to get there.

Let me unequivocally say this because many people have asked me whether I would do things over again if I had the chance: there's no fucking way I would go to law school again knowing what I know now. There's no way you can convince me that taking on the soul-crushing amount of debt is a good idea. My student loan debt was more than the GDP of some African countries. It's not a good idea. Don't do it. I'm not saying that because I don't want more competition in the legal field. I'm saying it because unless you have a fucking trust fund or some rich eccentric relative that's going to pay for everything, don't fucking go to law school.

But in 2002, I didn't know that. Had I done the proper amount of research, I probably could have found the answers that I needed to make the decision not to go, but it's one of those things - even if I had discovered those concerns, would I have listened? That's the real question. I feel that doing things the way that I did was meant to be. I was meant to go to Miami. I was meant to absolutely sweat my balls off for a year in the lawless swamp that is Florida. I played a lot of video games as a kid, so to borrow from them, this was part of my quest. The next level and achievement was to take place in Florida. It sounds crazy reading that now, Florida? What good ever happened in Florida?

I took a huge risk. I stepped out of my comfort zone. I hated the idea of being around large groups of people. But where did I go to law school? In a place where there are a ton of people, and a place where so many people travel to each year. I did something big. It may not have been the best decision for me to make, but I participated in the process of bettering myself by doing it. I could have stayed in East Lansing and thought small. I could have let my fears limit me, but 22-year-old me was on the right path. I may not have taken the right turn, but at least I was headed in the right direction. What was to come in Miami was like the process of forging steel. The heat of Miami and the pressure of law school would burn off those impurities that lingered inside of me. I was so immersed in everything that I didn't know that at the time, but looking at things from thirty thousand feet tells me, "Hey, at least you did something; some people never try at all."

Now that I have decided to go to Miami, I need a place to live. Jeff, the PI, drove my parents and me around, and we looked at a few places. I found one that was within walking distance of the school. The complex looked like the place that Daniel LaRussa from the Karate Kid lived. It was complete with an old Jewish woman from New Jersey and everything. I think that's what made me feel comfortable about it. She was the super for the building, and her husband, Saul, was the other point of contact. She insisted on calling me Nicholas, which was sweet at first, but got annoying because she'd use your name all of the time. Hello Nicholas. Goodbye, Nicholas. The rent is late, Nicholas. It got on my nerves.

I think I picked that place because I honestly didn't want to look at any more places. It was so goddamn hot outside that I just wanted to sit in an air-conditioned room and ice my balls. I also picked this place without my future wife's, Jules, approval. Now that we've been married for 19 years and together for over 20, she needs final approval on everything. She says it's because she's a Virgo, but I think it's because she knows deep down I'm a child. She's not wrong. To be honest, I at least should have sent her a pic of the apartment before I signed the lease, but I didn't want to engage in a conversation that you hear on a remodeling show. The apartment had everything that apartments need. It had a door, a couple of them, a toilet, a shower, and brown particle board paneling in the living room that was a disaster. Oh, and it did have a window unit air conditioner, so we wouldn't die. Why does it have to be so goddamn hot in Miami? The climate is like it doesn't want anyone to live there. I guess I was used to Michigan being like that.

One day in the late summer of 2002, Jules and I packed up all of our stuff and started the journey out of Michigan and into our new life in Miami. I should mention this about Jules. She is probably the most talented person that I've ever met. She has an incredible voice. Other than the fact that she was (and still is) a smoke show, her voice was the first thing that attracted me to her.

The first time that I saw her sing in college, I was blown away by how amazing she was. There's a brilliance in her voice, something that is indescribable and pure. I'm not that good of a writer, so I can't think of any other way to put into words what it feels like but it's the kind of classically trained voice that seems superhuman. It sounds corny as hell, but it does sound angelic.

Jules studied vocal performance at Michigan State. At that age, she was the kind of person who was incredibly talented and didn't have to work at all at her craft. She starred in many productions. She was so good that I actually went to them. It would take a lot to keep 20-year-old me from a night of drinking and playing video games, so you know that she had to be talented to keep me away from the High Life. Sure, it was opera, so it was mind-numbingly boring, but her voice made it tolerable. I could have given a shit less about the other people in the cast and what they were doing, but when she sang, it made me feel so good. I wanted to stand up and announce to everyone in the auditorium, "That's my girlfriend!"

I remember the first time she asked me to come to one of her performances. I hadn't heard her sing before. I knew she was a music major, but I didn't know that I was dating the Lebron James of opera. I was excited and also nervous because I didn't know anyone else there. I showed up and sat by myself in the back. It was a performance of "The Ballad of Baby Doe." I have no fucking clue what it was about. I'm fairly sure Jules was Baby Doe. She wasn't a deer, though. She was dressed up as a human. Whatever her role was, she came on stage and fucking nailed it. However, there was a male love interest in the performance, so as a 20-year-old immature male, I had pangs of jealousy. I felt sick, like when you drink too much Code Red Mountain Dew on an empty stomach and the red dye goes to work on your insides.

Every time I saw this guy holding her, I got more and more pissed. When they kissed, I was like "what the fuck?" She didn't give me a heads-up that was going to happen. Like George McFly, I wanted to interrupt the performance with "Get your damn hands off her!!!"

After the show, I told her that she was amazing and absolutely blew me away. Then I asked, calmly, who her scene partner was, the one that she sucked face with for like half an hour, but I did it all chill and stuff. She's like, "Oh, that's (some dude's name I don't remember). Don't worry, he's gay." It shouldn't have mattered, but WHEEW! I had never been so relieved to learn the sexual orientation of another man before. I was so excited, I wanted to make out with him.

After undergrad, Jules had a choice of what she wanted to do. She did very well in college and had plans to go to a music conservatory after that. That's where you do nothing but music, you're not fucking around with the b.s. classes you have to take in college. Jules is a soprano. Not like Tony Soprano. It's her voice type. They sing the high parts. Here's the thing about sopranos, there's a fucking million of them. It seems like 99% of female singers are sopranos. Why is that a big deal? Because there are only so many slots for female sopranos at music conservatories. Some schools may only take 5 or 6 sopranos every year, and that figure is high for the best music conservatories. The odds were not in her favor to be able to get into the schools that she wanted, but I, stupidly, underestimated her talent.

It turned out that Jules got into every music conservatory that she wanted. She got into Boston Conservatory, New England Conservatory and Peabody Conservatory. I had no idea how amazing these schools were but as an example, they're like the Princeton, Yale and Stanford of law schools. She had a decision to make. Which one would she choose? New England Conservatory

86

was in Boston, Peabody was in Baltimore, and Boston Conservatory was in, you guessed it, Boston.

As Jules tends to do, she blew me away with the decision that she made. She decided not to go to any of these schools. Out of the hundreds of female sopranos who applied to get into these slots, she made it and was selected. That put her in very elite company. Not many people can say that they got into one of these schools, let alone three. Then she did a very Jules thing and said, "Nah, I'm going to pass." She blew me away, again, with the amount of chutzpah she had by doing that.

She told me that the reason she did this was that she wanted to take a year off and come down to Miami with me. I told her that I was going to have no life whatsoever because I needed to do well in my first year of law school. She was cool with that. However, I knew that I was going to disappoint her because there's no way that I was going to be as available as she needed me to be. We were going to be living in a completely new place. We'd have no friends. I'd be studying my ass off, and she'd be alone. I asked her if she was able to reconsider. I could try and transfer up to where she was after a year, but she insisted that she needed a break from singing. It was an extremely competitive world with a lot of personalities. As I would soon find out, law was like that as well.

As we headed down to Miami, I had no idea what law school would be like. I had dreams of everyone hanging out with each other, engaging in intellectual discussions about legal theory and politics, and, for some reason, there was also a guy with a guitar playing "Classical Gas." I don't even know that piece very well; I just like to say it because it reminds me of an old fart.

When we eventually made it down to Miami, we were exhausted. The drive had taken two days, and we had eaten at several Cracker Barrels. By that time, I had perfected the golf tee game that you do while you wait at a Cracker Barrel. I learned that there's not a lot of diversity in the clientele at a Cracker Barrel (probably because of the name?) and, holy shit, old people love

Cracker Barrel. The place is littered with them. Old white people love bland ass food and stupid knick-knacks.

After we unpacked, we decided to go and get my books. There was a bookstore a few blocks away from our apartment on Santona, but we decided to drive because we're from the Midwest. I had my list of books. There were a ton of books. It was like I was starting my own little library. Both of us had our hands full and also had a shopping cart full of books. I had a lot of assigned reading in undergrad at Michigan State, but damn. This seemed excessive. Little did I know how much reading I would be doing for the next three years. Foreshadowing.

As we walked out of the bookstore, we were laughing at how many books we had. Our arms and hands were full of bags. The next thing that happened was we saw a tow truck back out of its parking spot and directly into my 1997 Chevrolet Monte Carlo. I had been a resident of Miami for not more than 5 hours, and already, some asshole had smashed my car. All I could do was drop my books and utter the words "What the fuck?!" Luckily, I guess, he was driving a tow truck.

This wasn't a little scratch that was going to buff out with some spit and an old t-shirt either. This was "oh damn" kind of damage. Two men jump out of the tow truck, and the passenger starts yelling at the driver in Spanish. I don't speak Spanish. My conversational Spanish is limited to food, specifically cheese, so unless we were all talking about pouring some cheese on my car to fix it, I had no idea what they were saying. They looked around in a way that you'd see in a silent movie, where the dude who did something wrong wanted to see if anyone saw what he did. They were like two Hamburglars and wanted to know if anyone else in McDonald land saw that they smashed my fucking car. If not, it looked like they were going to leave.

Luckily, they didn't leave because they saw me. They didn't know it was my car, but using their powers of deduction, they were able to see my "what the fuck, man?" look on my face and deduce it was my car. Instantly, their demeanor changed, and they came over and started speaking Spanish to me. I smiled and said slowly, "I have no idea what you're saying. No tiendo... No hablo Espanol." They both said "Oh" at the same time, which was weird. They couldn't have planned the timing any better. The driver pulled out his cell phone. I thought, "Thank you, we're going to call the police and get this sorted out."

He dials a number and starts speaking Spanish to the person on the other end. I was impressed. I had no idea that the police spoke Spanish down here. Now, I felt like I was the only one who didn't. The driver finishes his conversation with the person on the other end and hands me his phone. I say "Hello," and the person on the other end tells me that his name is Javy. Javy tells me that the driver of the tow truck is his brother, and he's in the U.S. illegally. If we get the police involved, he's going to get deported. Javy says that his brother has a repair shop, and he will tow my car there and fix the damage, and drive my car back to me. As Javy is telling me this, the driver is looking at me like I did to my parents after I asked them if we could get a puppy. His wide eyes and hopeful face were waiting for me to say, "Yes, let's do it."

I don't know why I did it, but I agreed to this. Looking back on it now, handing over my car to a total stranger who had just hit it doesn't seem like a great idea. I guess I was a different person back then. I still had that part of my soul that trusted people and wanted to give them the benefit of the doubt. I didn't want to get this guy in trouble; I just wanted my car fixed. He had a tow truck, he had a body shop. What could possibly go wrong here? If 40-year-old me were next to that me in the parking lot, I'd be saying, "Dude, you can't be serious. You're turning over the only piece of evidence to the person that hit you and probably would have left had you not been in the parking lot at that moment." But I did it anyway. Jules and I trusted this guy.

As soon as I said "okay" on the phone to Javy, the driver looked equal parts happy and relieved. "We fix, yes?" Yeah, dude, you're going to fix my car and bring it back to me. We exchanged information (I didn't even test the number to make sure it was the right one) and he hitched up my car that he just smashed and drove away to his shop (which may not have been real) and Jules and I were left in the bookstore parking lot. Just as I was about to say, "I guess we're walking home," the tow truck driver stopped, stuck his head out of the window, and said, "Get in." I still can't believe I did that, too. I've watched enough murder documentaries on Netflix to know that getting into some strange dude's car isn't a good idea. All four of us climbed in, and they drove us back to our new apartment on Santona. It felt good to be home.

A week later, the driver called Jules. I watched the two of them have a conversation on the phone. When she hung up, I asked is the car done? In a very confused way she looked at me and said "I guess?" A half hour later he called again and said "we're here." There was my car, as good as new. It turns out there are some good people left in the world. Although this was in the early 2000s, so maybe not anymore.

Class starts next week. The uncertainty of whether I'd see my car again provided a nice distraction from the beginning of law school. I had no idea what was going to happen. I got my schedule and it didn't look that difficult. I had Torts (I had no clue what that meant), Contracts (by that time, I'd signed a few of those), Criminal Procedure (ooh, that sounds gritty and raw), Legal Writing (that sounds gross, and Elements of Evidence (what the fuck does that mean?)

I would have preferred if all of the classes happened on one day. I'd be able to block out class that one day and then use the other 6 to get ready for the lectures. Unfortunately, my classes were staggered throughout the week, which meant that I'd be walking back and forth from my apartment to campus. Over the first month, this got too annoying and hot to accomplish. From experience, you can't learn the law when your body is producing enough sweat as a hot yoga class. It's uncomfortable and embarrassing to have sweat rings under your arms at 8am on a Monday morning for your first day of law school.

Luckily, the torts professor had something even more embarrassing than my pit stains happen to her. She was a middle aged woman with very elfish features. I should have been more excited to have her as a professor because now it seemed like I was student at Hogwarts rather than The University of Miami School of Law. I would have rather studied at Hogwarts. I probably would have been a Ravenclaw. Everyone wants to be Gryffindor, anything but Hufflepuff. You've seen the movies.

As she started to introduce herself to us and was explaining the syllabus, I noticed a spot on her left breast. I didn't think anything of it at first and I continued to listen as she explained page two of the syllabus. I was beginning to freak out when I saw how many pages of reading were assigned for each class. I had 80 pages to read before Wednesday. Having looked at the book before the first day, I could tell that it wasn't going to be a page turner like "The Prisoner of Azkaban," there weren't even any pictures in these books!

I looked up again and the spot on her left breast was bigger than it was before. I already felt uneasy recovering from the sweatiest walk I've ever been through to get to class. Now it appeared that my professor's left breast was leaking. I thought to myself "What the fuck is happening here?" I had so many questions already, now I wondered if I should say something. "Professor, your breast appears to be leaking, just wanted to bring that to your attention." Or do I do the thing where I cough and then point to my left breast as if to say "hey, there's a situation happening there that you might want to pay attention to." I did nothing and sat in a confused silence and the spot on her boob got bigger.

At that moment, the guy sitting at the desk immediately in front of me turned around, looked at me with a raised eyebrow as if to say "are you seeing this shit?" Later, I would learn his name was

Mike and his friendship helped me get through my first year of law school in Miami.

I never really knew what the fuck happened. I don't have functioning breasts, mine are just for show. So I don't know if she was lactating or what. Not to seem rude, but she seemed kinda old to be breastfeeding. If I were to picture her kid, it would be a dude in his 20s and for the love of God I would hope that she wouldn't still be breastfeeding a kid at that age. That'd be like "Hey mom, I had a hard day at college. Oh I'm sorry, baby. Have a suckle on mom's left tete and tell me all about it." In a world where grown people dress up like animals and fuck, yes I'm looking at you furries, I guess anything's possible. But also "eww."

After that weird lecture, I wasn't sure if my other professors could top that. Turns out they couldn't. After torts, which is basically the law that allows you to sue someone. Like if you slip and fall or your neighbor's dog bites you or your neighbor's dog bites you and then you slip and fall and you sue your neighbor (AWKWARD!) then you're using the principles that I learned in torts.

After torts, I had to go to contracts. My professor for this was a middle aged dude named Michael Fishl. I was quite sure that he didn't have a set of working female breasts so I would be able to pay attention to the lecture and not to his leaking left breast. Michael Fishl was generally an okay professor. He would throw in pop culture references like lyrics to Ben Fold's Five songs. When he talked about the concept of restitution, he said it made him think of the lyrics "give me my money back, give me my money back, you bitch." I'd never heard a Professor say the word bitch before, so that was kind of cool.

The one thing that stuck in my craw about ol' Mike Fishl was this: he made us buy a book that he wrote for his class. Taking myself back to 2002, I was prepared to do anything to succeed in law school. It was a confusing time. Law school is teaching you how to think like a lawyer, which, all jokes aside for a second, is

92

completely different than how I had viewed the world up until that point in my life. I used to see things positively. Now I'm fairly sure I'm dead inside. My point is, back in 2002 when a professor gives me a syllabus and they put a book on it, I'm going to read that book.

However, as I would discover later by going to his lectures, he never talked about that fucking book. At. All. I read that stupid book "Getting to Maybe" because my professor told me to and then at the last class of the semester he finished up and as everyone was gathering their things I looked around like "when are we going to talk about that book you wrote that you had us buy?" I felt like a total rube. He's sitting there counting the 15 bucks that I had to drop on it and laughing manically. What a great scam. You got me, Fischl. You're an authority figure and as part of your curriculum you tell your students to read particular books because it's going to teach them about Contracts. Who wrote that book? Why me of course! It's a great racket. I gotta put myself in a position to be able to do shit like that. That's like a judge gives you a list of things to do before your sentencing to prepare and at the bottom of the list he wrote buy this tabletop grill and it turns out that the judge owns the company.

I should have known this was a rouse. I fell for this kind of shit in college, too. But in law school you had a finite amount of time to be able to read to prepare for each class. I barely had enough time to read everything as it was. There were times like I felt like I was a failure because I wasn't able to get all of the reading done beforehand. Then Mike Fischl comes in with his curly fucking hair and his stupid book with his dumb face on the book jacket and steals from me the time that I could have used to figure out what the fuck they were writing about in Hadley v. Baxendale. Yeah, so that was contracts. As you can tell, I'm still a little salty about that.

The professor that, by far, made the most impact on me was the person that taught this class called Elements. I showed up on the first day, not having any clue what to expect. Elements? I don't want to learn about Zinc, I need to know how to sue someone, dammit! I saw that the professor for Elements wrote the book for this class too, so after the whole Fishl debacle, forgive me if I was a bit skeptical.

The time comes for class and we're all sitting there waiting for class to start. A couple of minutes late, this guy walks down the aisle to the front of the class. His hair looks like he just stuck his head under one of those gas station hand dryers and it's a mess. It's completely white. He's not carrying anything. He had to be the professor but he didn't have any books or notes or anything. I had no idea what was going to happen.

He starts to speak and he's one of those people that when he speaks you lean in and listen to what he has to say. It's a combination of cadence and volume and facial expression. There aren't many people like that I've encountered but he was one of them. He knew exactly what the assigned reading was and what it was covering. This class would be my first experience with the Socratic Method.

If you don't know what the Socratic Method is, then you've probably lived a much less stress-free existence than I and all other people that have gone to law school. The idea is that the professor isn't the one that's doing the instruction. The professor merely asks questions of the students and relies upon them to respond. As the dialogue continues, the professor asks more and more specific questions of the student until the point of the original question is made clear for everyone.

Hold up, you mean that the professor isn't the one doing the teaching, they're just answering questions? Yeah, that's exactly what I mean. I know what you're thinking, this sounds like another bamboozle, a hustle. It kind of is and it kind of isn't. When Terrence J. Anderson showed up with no book for that first Elements class he knew exactly what he was talking about. He knew it so well that mother fucker didn't even need a book or notes or a power point presentation. He just showed up.

94

After a brief introduction about himself which wasn't braggy at all, he points at this dude in the second row and asks him "what is the holding of *(some case that I can't remember)*." Oh shit, this dude got called on the first day of class. My asshole immediately clenched up for him. I started to go into panic mode because I had read the material but I hadn't READ the material, you what I mean, fam?

I felt bad for this dude for a number of reasons. This was our first day of law school and up until that point, I had heard about the Socratic Method but I hadn't seen it in action. The guy that got called on had a very hateable face. I'm sure you've encountered someone like that in your life. He looked like he came from New England and he had curly hair on top and before class he was talking a lot and seemed very braggadocious. Now he was getting his comeuppance because ol' T-Dawg Anderson (aka Terry Anderson or just T - these were the names I had given him in my head) was handing his ass to him.

That day I learned how not to respond when you're called on in law school. This dude, let's call him Brice, because his name was probably Brice, was so fucking arrogant I was taken aback. Now I've reached a point in my life where I've dealt with all kinds of people and we each have different reactions to stress. Some people get all quiet. Some people run. Some people shit their pants. Some people act like an asshole. Brice was the kind of person that acted like an asshole.

The verbal battle between Brice and Terrence Anderson didn't last long. It was like when I was a kid I'd see Mike Tyson fight a white toll booth operator. Brice v. T-Dawg Anderson was like that. There weren't any referees. Professor Anderson knew when the Brice had enough. He didn't even tell him to stop, he just raised his hand and Brice stopped talking. Real power move. Professor Anderson had the kind of energy that Robert California had in "The Office." He may be crazy, but he may also be a genius. I didn't know. I did know that I needed to fucking prepare for next class because I didn't want to enjoy the fate which had befallen Brice. RIP, Brice.

After that class, we'd never see Brice again. I assume that he decided that law school wasn't right for him. At the time, I laughed because he couldn't cut it. He was an asshole so he probably felt like he didn't deserve to be treated like that. I don't know. Now I wonder whether Brice was the lucky one. As he stood in front of the entire class looking like a jerkoff, did he see the future and saw an opportunity to jump out of the plane before it hit Normandy? Sometimes when I least expect it, I think about Brice. We were all driving down the same road that one day and he decided to jerk the wheel and took a left and it ended up taking over his dad's Hyundai dealership. We all kept going straight, each of us for different reasons.

After Professor Anderson dismantled Brice, it was time for lunch. The schadenfreude that I experienced during those 55 minutes was a high point in an otherwise weird and shitty morning. This can't be how it is, right? Being thrown into the deep end and being expected to swim can't be the way we teach people to be lawyers. Little did I know that it was exactly how we teach people to be lawyers. The events of this morning were simply a harbinger of what was to come over the next 3 years.

I exited the Elements classroom confused. I needed to get lunch so I went to "The Cafe" I got a sandwich wrapped in plastic wrap and dropped myself into the plastic chair, built for looks rather than comfort. At that time, cell phones really weren't a thing like they are now so I just had to sit there with my sad plastic wrapped bullshit and my thoughts.

Then out of nowhere, this tall athletic guy sits down at the table next to me. It was Ken Dorsey. If you don't know who Ken Dorsey was, you're not alone. He was the quarterback for the University of Miami Football team. At that time, to be the QB for the Hurricanes was a pretty big deal. It was weird, he was sitting alone as well. I was expecting that he would have an entourage of hangers on come and sit with him for lunch but that never happened. He sat at a table alone just like me. I wondered what he was studying. He was probably having a different experience from my morning. Unless he was also in Torts, I can guarantee that none of his professors had a leaky left tit. He looked over and I did that thing that guys do to seem tough yet acknowledge each other's existence, I nodded my head and he nodded his.

After I sat in silence with just my thoughts, I walked to my last class of the day, criminal procedure. At the time, I had no interest in anything to do with criminal law. I thought it was the low hanging fruit of the law, nothing particularly challenging about it. I sat on the right side of the class a few rows up. I waited for my professor to bore me for an hour, possibly humiliate me or some other Brice-like kid and then go home and take a nap.

In walks a dark haired woman in her early 30s. She walked to the front of the room and told us that she was going to teach criminal procedure differently than most professors did. I was like "ok good, because some of these other professors seem like they're on some bullshit." Her first "lecture" was like the rest of them that followed that semester. It was essentially a masterclass on how the government is bad and is trying to take away your civil rights. It was like every Monday and Wednesday afternoon she turned a Rage Against the Machine song into a lecture.

The content was uber-liberal for it's time. I'm a liberal, but damn. The stuff she was talking about was out there. It felt like this lecture was the first in a three part plan to turn us all into Zapatista rebels. "Hey Jules, I'm going to take a class trip and I'll be gone for a while. We're going to help this indigenous tribe overthrow their oppressors."

I don't think I learned one fucking thing about criminal procedure. Sure, the lectures were a real hoot. However, I learned more in one hour of practicing criminal defense than a semester of criminal procedure. I did learn that George W. Bush was a fascist pig. However, I found that piece of knowledge doesn't really translate into the practice of law. I hope she's well. I'm sure she's fighting the power while driving her Audi and living in South Beach.

Seriously, if you're going to teach a law school class, you gotta get your shit together. Teach me something. Teach me what an arraignment is and what the purpose of it is, I didn't move 1,400 miles to learn how Dick Cheney is the puppet master and we're just a cog in the machine of injustice. Anyway, as she wrapped up her commie propaganda, and I mean that nicely, we could close the book on day 1 of law school.

I walked home and as always in Miami, I sweat my ass off. I entered our little apartment on Santona soaking wet, said "hi" to Jules and headed straight to the bathroom to take a shower. While I had learned the therapeutic value of a shower beer in college, I decided to not imbibe. I think it was because I had 9,834 pages to read before my next class and I was exhausted.

Jules wanted to know how it went. Her face was way too excited when she asked this. She had the same childlike whimsical notions of what law school that I did before 8am that morning. I told her that it was pretty rough. I shared with her the Brice story and in true comedic structure, I ended with a bang and shared the tale of the leaky left breast. She hugged me and it felt good to have human contact. I felt like I had been in space for a year and needed to acclimate myself back into real society. Thankfully, the air conditioner was working and we had a bed because I took one of the greatest afternoon naps in human history.

I woke up in same way that I would wake up throughout my law school career, in a panic. There was so much to do and there was no way to get it all done. Looking back on things, I should have come up with a system to block out time. From this time to this time, I'll read torts, at this time I'll read property, and for this hour I'll hug myself and cry in the closet.

While day one was overwhelming, day 2 was uneventful. I only had one class that was called Legal Writing. It was taught at six thirty at night, which was bullshit. There's no need to teach a law school class in the evening. There are specific programs for people who are going to law school and working at the same time. Sidenote, props to you if you did that because that must have been an accomplishment. I barely got through law school I couldn't imagine having a real job on top of that during the first year. I was able to support myself through student loans. It was the early 2000s and everyone thought that the economy would continue to expand and by the end of 2005 I would be walking down the street and be able to shit nickels. Spoiler alert, that didn't happen.

I'll spare you the blow by blow details of my semester in legal writing but suffice it to say that my professor was the worst teacher I've ever had and also claimed the prize as the biggest asshole. She was in her early 30s and was a clerk for a judge in Miami. That's why we had to have the class at 6:30pm - let's inconvenience 30 people so it can fit with one person's schedule. That's the way judges do it, so maybe she was getting us ready to be lawyers. She gave us no lecture whatsoever, which really called having to have this class at 6:30pm into question. She came up with hypothetical situations with fact patterns and wanted us to write legal briefs for her. Mind you, at that point I'd never written a legal brief before and I can safely say that no one else in my class did either. Why? Because we'd never been to law school. I had no fucking clue what to do. The first class was basically her stupid ass handing out the syllabus and giving us the peace out sign. You could tell she was overworked and she was also pregnant, so I get that she was busy (or at least she had been getting busy - ay oh!) but this is still a class that we're paying for. Teach us something, bud!

I did not do well in Legal Writing. A combination of things attributed to that. First, I didn't like confrontation. 40 year old me would have felt more confident to talk to this jerk after class and say "Umm, hi, can you teach us something next time?" However, I fell into the trap of thinking that this was an authority figure and they know best. In reality, she was just trying to skate by and pick up a paycheck to be able to get a nice crib for this baby that was due in the Spring.

It wasn't just that I didn't do well. It was the way in which I felt broken after each assignment. I had always done well in college and in high school. If I didn't do well, I was at least on the right track and a teacher would show me how to do better next time. This class was a one hour dismantling of the self-esteem that I had built up over the last 23 years. The professor would stand her pregnant ass up in front of the class and talk about how all of our briefs were crap. However, she didn't have any suggestions how to make them better. That's the worst kind of teaching. Teaching legal writing is more than having a red pen. If you don't have a plan as to how to get someone to do better, then you might as well not even be teaching. I know this now, but then I was a scared kid who thought there was something wrong with me because I wasn't getting it. Looking back, this was the beginning of the metamorphosis from semi-happy Nick to the overly anxious and angry Nick.

Law school is people telling you how you should be learning how to think like a lawyer. It's like a tradition passed down and passed down over time. Unfortunately, it's all bullshit. This woman thought she had to be a certain way because that's how her legal writing teacher was, a real stupid asshole. She had no business being a teacher or any demonstrable legal skills herself. She decided to take a position in the legal writing program to inflict the pain that someone had inflicted on her when she was in law school. It's unfortunate and sad. There's an opportunity to shape the minds of thousands of people each day who have made the decision to be lawyers and institutions are failing. Training you to become a lawyer doesn't have to be this Spartan experience where they try and find the weakest and throw them off a cliff. But so many think it has to be that way because they experienced this systematic deconstruction of personality that they see it is their job to perpetuate the bullshit.

My legal writing professor could have shown us how she wanted our papers to look like. She could have shown us examples of her legal writing and used that as a tool - here's what I did here, here's where I could have tightened this up and this is how not to do things. But she didn't.

I should have had the courage within me to call her out on this bullshit, but I didn't. And that's okay, because I wasn't ready to do that at the time. I was going through something. I didn't know what it was at the time, and I still don't know what it was. But I put myself into the meat grinder that was law school and came out the other end a different person. In some ways I was better, and other ways I was worse. I thought that being a lawyer was what I wanted to be without ever really examining the why. I never looked at what it would mean to be a lawyer, I was simply looking at what was in front of my face. It's like saying I like playing around with rockets without considering at the end of becoming an astronaut you're going to be in space. Do you really want to be in space? You should probably figure out if that's a good fit for you before you start flipping upside down in that gyroscope thingy. But I didn't do any of that. I was in the space shuttle and they were counting down from ten. There was no turning back.

The Morning of Trial

The drive to the courthouse is 27 minutes. Before my life was ruined with the law, I was passionate about music. What better music for the first day of a murder trial than DMX? As I make the turns onto the highway, I sing out loud in my car "Y'all gonna make me lose my mind, up in here, up in here." When I get to the last red light before the highway, I stop yelling DMX lyrics. There's a black homeless man on the side of the road and I'm as full of white guilt as I am of gout.

After the third replay of DMX's opus, I arrive at the courthouse. I pull into the space where I always park my car. It's the furthest one away because I don't want any d-bags scratching the paint of my Altima. Even if there's no one in the parking lot I park there because I want to make it look like I tried to get 10,000 steps in a day. More importantly, my ass needs more time to dry out before I must interact with another human.

I walk up the 8 concrete stairs to the county building and the automatic door opens for me, then the next one opens. There's no going back now. Like my buddy Chris Simpson says when he runs a yellow light "we're committed." The quick walk from my car to the building helped burn off a bit of the anxiety. I say hello to one of the sheriff's deputies who's running security. They know me so

I don't have to disrobe like the other plebs (now I am bragging, I hate going through security, probably because I think they'll discover I have a sweaty ass). The metal detector thing buzzes and we chit-chat for a second and the deputy tells me "good luck!" In a very Larry Davidian way I interpret that as him wishing me anti-luck and I push the button for the elevator.

I hate this elevator because it makes me feel like a husky lad. Even if it's just me on the elevator, it really moves around when you step inside. I can tell you that's not what you want your elevator to do. I need my elevators to be the strong silent type. I'm the one that's wobbling about, not you, elevator. I push the button to the 4th Floor "Circuit Court." As I always do, I notice the button for the 3rd floor marked "Prosecuter." The misspelling makes me worry about the quality control of this elevator. If they're not spell checking their signs, it makes me think that there are some important parts that are probably missing.

After my tense ride, I arrived on the fourth floor and stepped off the elevator. I was thankful that I was on solid ground again. I'm confronted with a wall of humanity. The hallway is filled with potential jurors. They're doing what I normally do when I occupy this space, pace nervously up and down the hallway. From their looks, I can't tell if they know if I'm the lawyer for the prosecution or the defense, but I got that "he's a lawyer" vibe from them. I didn't like it. It wasn't my fault that these people had to take off work to be here. Get pissed at the prosecutor, he's the one that thought this murder was a big deal.

I walk through the narrow path that they've left in the hallway and enter through the double doors to the courtroom. The clerk is sitting at her computer up front. She greets me with a "Good morning, Nick!" and a sheriff's deputy does the same. It's not been a particularly good morning for me so far. My ass was operating at an approximate 70% humidity index at that moment. No one else is in the courtroom but us three. It's way too quiet. I can feel that they want to chit chat, but I can also sense that they want to leave me alone to prepare. I appreciate that. There's nothing like someone who loves to talk incessantly when they're in a nervous situation. I put my bag down on the big wooden desk. I have no way of knowing, but it looks like oak. It looks and feels solid. I start pulling books, notepads, and pens and begin arranging them on the desk. There's a brass plate on the back of one of the two chairs at the table that explains that Amish people made the desk and chairs. That confuses me. I've never seen an Amish in court before. I guess that makes sense because they're not getting pulled over for drunk driving in a horse and buggy. If you're into boozin' and cruisin', that's probably one of the perks of being Amish. Chances are, if you do see an Amish person in court, they must have done some pretty fucked up shit, like killed another Amish dude for sleeping with their wife. "You don't churn another man's butter, Ezekiel!" and then he hits him with a wooden mallet that he carved out of one piece of wood. Anyway, if you see an Amish in court, I'd recommend giving them a wide berth.

I was moving around a bit and it made me feel less anxious. The deputy asked me if I wanted to see my client. "Did I want to see him or do I need to see him?," I thought. I said "sure," because I wanted to go over one last time that I needed him to not do anything stupid in court. I know all he had to do was sit there and look not guilty, but having read my client's criminal history, he did have a history of playing loosey-goosey with the rules.

The deputy took me in the back and I felt like I was backstage at a play. It seemed like any minute I was going to see the actual wheels of justice turning. I felt strange being back there and was glad that he was walking me to where I had to go. The deputy told me which room my client was going to be in, and I went inside and sat down. There was plexiglass between me and the other side and it felt cold in there because everything was painted cinder block. It was painted white and it looked like the interior decorator said "let's make this room look really creepy." On the other side of the plexiglass was a bench and a toilet. I've seen many clients in that room before. The time I'll never forget is when I had to see a client before his sentencing hearing and the deputy told me he had him set up waiting in the room already. That made me excited. Normally, I have to wait for them to go get the clients that are in jail so the deputy was saving me some time that morning and I appreciated it. When I opened the door, my client was on the toilet taking a shit. I know that because his face had the look of someone who just had someone walk in on him taking a shit. I said what I always say in moments like that, the classic midwestern "Ope!" I quickly closed the door. From behind the door I yelled, "I'll give you a few minutes." I walked back into the courtroom to wait because I didn't want to listen to another man taking a shit. The deputy asked what I was doing and I said he's busy at the moment. The deputy looked down at the monitor in front of him that had a video feed of every cell and said, "Yeah, it looks like he's taking a dump." Thanks, dude. You could have told me that.

Flashback to the alleged murderer. I was grateful he wasn't taking a shit when I walked into the visitation room. You could say I was relieved that he was not relieving himself. Ay-Oh! He was sitting on the opposite side of the plexiglass and was wearing the clothes that I had bought him. Yes, you heard that right. I bought him clothes. It seems like I should mention that we weren't in some sort of romantic relationship. It's not like he and I took an afternoon trip to Brooks Brothers and had a chocolate malted. I just bought him clothes. No strings attached.

I bought them at the Goodwill store in Dewitt, Michigan. I had asked my client's family if they could bring some clothes for him to the jail, and they never did. It was sad. They lived in Lansing, which is about 27 minutes away, and they couldn't bring up any clothes for their brother or son, who was on trial for murder. It made me feel sorry for my client. The people who were the closest to him seemingly couldn't care less about him. Conversely, it made me feel pretty lucky to have a family that has supported me throughout the years. I'm fairly sure that if I were on trial for murder, my wife would bring clothes for my trial to the jail. My client's family didn't. This meant that I had two choices - 1) he would show up for his murder trial wearing the faded yellow uniform that they give to inmates with "County Jail" stenciled in black spray paint on the back with the standard issue pair of orange knock off Crocs, OR 2) I could go buy my client clothes at the Goodwill in Dewitt, Michigan. I chose the latter.

I'd never bought clothes for another man before. When I got to the Goodwill, I also realized that I forgot to ask the alleged murderer what size pants, shirt, and shoes he wore. Those are kind of important details when you're shopping for clothes. It's not like I could have brought him to the Goodwill with me. "Hey guys, we're headed to the Goodwill. I'll have this rascal back before chow time!" At this point, I should mention that he and I were completely different-sized people. I would have totally let this guy borrow some of my clothes; however, he was about 5'4", or whatever height Kevin Hart is. I'm much larger than that.

I was in Goodwill for about 45 minutes just walking around, looking lost, like a man trying to find an anniversary present for his wife. Then it hit me. I always liked the show "Project Runway" and "Queer Eye," so this was my chance to give this guy a makeover. I couldn't let my client wear the clothes he was wearing when he was arrested, because he looked super murdery in those. I had to strike a balance between business casual and totally innocent.

A middle-aged woman who worked at the Goodwill must have noticed my confusion. She walked up and asked, "Can I help you?" I'm like, "Oh, I'm just looking for some clothes for a client." Immediately after saying that, I realized that this lady probably didn't know that I meant by "client." She was probably thinking, "Oh, this bald pimp is just here getting some clothes for some of his male escorts."

I think her name was Pam. She was really good at helping me find clothes. I found a shirt that looked like it was going to fit the tiny man who was my client. I got a bluish tie with a checkered pattern on it. I remembered hearing that blue is the color that you should wear when you want someone to think that you didn't murder a drug dealer. I got him some black pants and some shiny black shoes. I didn't get him any underwear, because while I'm very comfortable with my sexuality, I draw the line at buying another dude underwear. I paid and I felt like I did a good deed. I did something that this guy's family wouldn't even do for him. I also saved the receipt because I was totally going to write this off on my taxes.

After my successful shopping trip, I went to the jail and dropped off the clothes at the front desk to have them put in his property. The next time I saw the clothes was when my client walked into the room wearing them. I thought he looked good, and I felt like the mother of a middle schooler who picked out clothes for her son for the middle school dance. My client didn't look as pleased with the results. "What's with these clothes?" he asked. "Have you seen the jury?" I retorted. "We gotta make you blend in," I said, feeling upset that he was judging my sense of style. This was the best I could do. This was a bunch of white people. If they had had a Travis Tritt t-shirt with an eagle and an American flag on it, I would have gone for it. Pair that with a pair of camouflage pants, and he would have looked not guilty.

I don't remember what we talked about in that room, but I think it was me nervously rambling. I do remember him asking me for like the thousandth time "what do you think is gonna happen?" I wanted to say listen man 4 people said that they saw you shoot a dude, what the fuck do you think is gonna happen? Instead, I said, "I've worked hard for the last few months putting together the best defense I could under the circumstances." I paused and was proud of how lawyerly that sounded.

I confirmed with him one last time that he was not going to testify. That one took some convincing over many, many, many visits and letters.

There are two schools of thought when it comes to having your client testify. Some lawyers think that it's a way for your client to demonstrate to the jury that they're a real person who has their own side of the story and emotions. Other lawyers think that this is no time for your client to be talking because even if you've prepped them on what to avoid saying, there's no telling what's going to happen when the prosecutor has a chance to cross-examine them. My theory with this client was that he could be persuasive but not in a courtroom. Does that make sense? If I could have duct-taped his mouth shut without the jury noticing it, that's what I would have done. There's nothing that this guy would have been able to say that was going to help. It would have been a cluster fuck. In the end, he said that he wasn't going to testify because he trusted me. That's nice, an alleged murderer trusts my legal advice. That one's going to get added to the website and my resume tomorrow morning.

The Day I Was On Call For An Entire Class

The day before my next Elements class I read everything Professor Anderson assigned to us. No pictures or funny diagrams. Just tens of thousands of words arranged in an excruciatingly boring way. The assigned reading was a series of cases that involved people who were tenants in low-income housing in Washington, DC in the 1980s. They were getting shit on by their landlord. Plumbing and important things like heat in their apartments weren't being repaired. What was happening behind these cases was interesting and sad but there was no time for emotions, just read.

This lecture was the moment when I figured out what law school was all about. Professor Anderson and his crazy ass just told us to read those cases. I read them. And then I stepped back for a minute to see why he wanted us to read them. How did they fit together? How were they each similar? How were they different? That's the kind of next level thinking people probably did on a regular basis in college but I was very by the book and only did what I was told to do.

After reflecting on these cases, it wasn't like I figured anything out. No lightbulbs went on in my head. I was just as lost as I was when I began reading them. However, I started on a different path than I was on. I had branched off into another level of critical thinking that I hadn't really engaged in before. It would become like a muscle, it would get stronger with each time I used it.

After reading all of those cases and having to sort out all the pieces of how they worked together, I was exhausted. It's weird that you can feel exhausted when you're just reading for hours in your apartment. It wasn't like I was running a marathon or anything, I was just sitting there. But my brain was telling me, you're tired, you need to relax. This new path of critical thinking would also lead me down the path of getting fat and lazy. I told myself I worked really hard so I deserve a break, which meant more sitting. Ten years later, I looked at myself in the mirror and I looked fat and unhappy.

I walked into the Elements classroom and took the same seat I had the first day. This time Professor Anderson walked in and had a sheet of paper. It turns out it had all of our names written on it. I learned that it at least had my name on it when without warning he said "Mr. Leydorf, what can we learn from this series of cases?" Oh shit, this dude just called on me. No foreplay whatsoever, we're doing this.

As I started to form a word with my mouth, Professor Anderson did that very Professor Anderson thing and used his hand and raised it motioning me to stand. It was like he was Darth Vader and I was a Storm Trooper and he was using the force to make my ass stand up without words. It worked. I stood up in front of an entire class. At that moment, I had no idea that I would be standing up for the entire class. I also had no idea that at the end of class I would have taken a massive leap in personal growth and development. All I knew was that I was absolutely terrified and my nether regions began to perspire.

"Well, I think.." I said nervously and with a break in my voice that I get when I haven't yet talked to anyone that day. He interrupted and said one of the things that has stuck with me most from law school. "Mr. Leydorf, in this class we think in a LOUD voice." It was hilarious and I laughed. I don't know if he meant it to be funny. Professor Anderson had a deadpan sense of humor. He was doing that for my benefit. He knew I was scared. He didn't know me before he called on me but once he used the force to make me stand up he could tell that I was scared.

There are times in my life where I felt in complete control. I can count on my hands the number of times that I have experienced that feeling. Standing in front of that class was one of those times. The other times that I have felt it was when felt in the groove doing stand up. I become very aware of my surroundings but with tunnel vision at the same time. Words become effortless. I lose all sense of time. And I start sweating, the kind of sweat that you get from a morning jog. It's cold but kind of refreshing and pours out of the top of my head.

I don't remember much of exactly what I said, but I do remember some of the shifts in body language that Professor Anderson made after I answered some of his questions. I was able to gauge from his reaction that he knew he wasn't dealing with someone who was cut of the same cloth as that Brice character. I was someone who is approaching this material from a place of humility and who was demonstrating a desire to learn. I'm sure that there were some things that I said that made completely no sense whatsoever. I don't want to make it sound like after the class ended everyone applauded and a girl came up and kissed my cheek. It wasn't like that. But I felt a shift in the room. Some pieces were moving around for me for the better. I know I had to have done better than Brice because Brice got the hook after a couple of minutes. I had no idea I had handled 50 minutes worth of questions but he stopped and told us what we needed to read before next class. There was no "atta boy!" from Professor Anderson but I could tell that I was able to hold my own with Darth Vader and he didn't use the force to choke my ass out.

I remained standing with a "what the fuck just happened?" face. I looked around as everyone was gathering their things. I felt tingles in my forearms and fingers. I packed up and walked out of the air conditioned room and felt the extreme shock of the blistering heat. It would become that element that would ground me throughout that year. After each class I would step back out into reality. Looking back, I needed more of that reality check. I needed to take a break. Like a homicide detective, I was too close to these cases and needed to step back and look at everything from 30,000 feet.

Voir Dire

I get up and leave the attorney-client room and walk back through the faded white hallway again, but no one is out there. Maybe it's over and the prosecutor decided that he didn't want to go through with the case? Wishful thinking? Yes, but my brain usually works through even the minutiae to see if it's possible to avoid a 3 week trial. "What if there's a swarm of bees and they have to move the trial out a few weeks so that we can negotiate with the bees and hear their demands?" I walk back through the double doors and realize where all of the people went. They're now sitting in the courtroom. It was a shocking amount of people. They were eerily quiet, like when people try and surprise you for a birthday party. Which, by the way, I never understood. We all care about you enough to be here, but we're also going to scare the crap out of you. The cast of characters in the benches look like the people in the audience of Judge Judy. Which, sidenote, is my favorite legal show. As a lawyer, it's like the food at a Chinese buffet to me. I know it's not good for me, but I can't get enough of it.

The people are sitting there waiting for the show to start. They are nervously chit-chatting amongst themselves. A few, like I would be, are just sitting there actively trying to avoid being sucked into a shallow chit-chat conversation and would prefer to be left the fuck alone. Those are my kind of people. I should note that they're all white people. There's about 60 of them. Their ages range from early 20s to "holy shit that guy's old" years old. My client is not white. Many of the witnesses who will testify are not white. This county is predominantly white so the whole "jury of your peers" thing is not going to happen in this trial. I feel like that's one of the many areas of law where some old white guys said some shit hundreds of years ago and we just keep running with it even though we have the ability to make things different. We're on our first Constitution in this country and Italy has had more constitutions than a fraternity has VD scares. My point is we have the ability to make things different so let's look at that for about 10 minutes. That's all it would take to make a few things better for millions of people.

I sit at the desk and I am nervously shuffling my papers. I'm aware that there are 60 strangers behind me, judging me. Imagine doing your job and there are 60 people watching what you're doing. It's not very relaxing. I feel all of them staring at that spot behind my right ear. I hear the doors behind me open and the prosecutor and the officer in charge of the case walk in. The prosecutor is younger than me and has a full head of thick black hair (bastard!). He's pulling a piece of luggage like he's going on a trip. Inside are the piles of evidence that they have against my client. The officer is wearing a shirt and tie. The color combo reminds me of what Dwight Shrute from Dunder Mifflin would wear. Grey and mustard yellow shouldn't go together, I've watched enough "Project Runway" to know that. If you're counting, this is the second "Project Runway" reference. They walk in slow motion up to the swinging doors that separate the gallery from the judge and the lawyers. They look in my direction and give a half-hearted smile, the one where you raise your eyebrows and nod your head. I smile back and say "good morning." To be honest, though, I didn't really mean it.

It would have been nice to have someone else there with me as a second pair of eyes. Someone to help me go through some deep breathing and give an inspiring pep talk or two. But when you're getting paid dogshit, you have a house payment, a kid, and a mountain of student loan debt, there's not a lot of room in the budget to pay someone to be there every day in court to sit next to you and help you out.

What happens next is kind of a blur. The deputy walks up and says he is going to bring my client out. I say something unintelligible, something between an "okay" and an "alright," I believe it was "alkay." The level of anxiety is building. There's a ringing in my ears. Ass sweat concentration has reached 73% and is climbing. They bring out my client wearing the clothes I bought him and I look around to see the audience's reaction. I proudly wanted to declare "I picked those out," like a dad proudly showing his spouse the clothes he picked out for his son "all by himself." Like so many times in my life, I thought better of it. It would have been funny though.

At that moment, I looked down and caught a glimpse of a large steel ring under the table. Were they going to handcuff my guy to that ring? That's not going to be a good look, I told myself. "Hey, I know this guy is innocent, but he can be a real handful, so we're going to lock him to this table for the entire trial if that's cool with you?" Again, just to reiterate, he's totally innocent until proven guilty." The deputy doesn't handcuff him to the metal ring thingy. I'm relieved. But then it sinks in "Nick, there's an alleged murderer sitting next to you." Hey, on second thought, chief, can we chain this dude up over here? I have spent my life flipping back and forth from trying to look and be the stereotypical "strong, silent type" and being an emotional wreck. Usually, I can walk the wire, balancing the two artfully. However, with my anxiety at an 11 out of 10 and having a sweaty ass, I was struggling like a motherfucker to hold on.

My inner struggle is interrupted as the judge walks through the open door to the left of the courtroom. Simultaneously, the deputy says "all rise" in a kind but stern tone. The judge walks through the doors and up the few steps to the bench. She's wearing a long robe so you can't see her feet. It's like she's floating to where she wants to go. I wish I could float on out of this courthouse, go home, and throw all of my lawyer paraphernalia away. Briefcase? Trash. Suits? Garbage. Files? Set those fuckers on fire! I'd have a couple of shower beers and try and wash the gritty exterior that being a lawyer left on my skin. It'd done a number on me, and I wanted it all to go away.

This particular judge is one of my favorite judges. That's like having a favorite dentist. It's never fun working with them, but some make it more enjoyable than others. She's always treated me with kindness. That's something that is often lost in the profession. Lawyers are too focused on being right and winning than they are on being a fucking human being. That's one reason why I usually can't be friends with lawyers, because they always want to talk about their conquests, like the hunter who killed an elephant, he's totally oblivious of the destruction that his "win" caused.

Being a judge has to be an exceedingly difficult and stressful job. Honestly, becoming a judge is what I wanted to do all of those years ago when I decided that I wanted to be a lawyer. Back up, that's not true. Writing this has exposed how deeply concerned I am with how I am perceived by others. Upon further examination, I wanted to be a judge first. Then, when I found out that you had to be a lawyer to be a judge, I figured out that I wanted to become a lawyer. What's interesting is how becoming a judge got lost through undergrad and law school. As I soldiered on, I convinced myself that I'll never be able to become a judge. I wasn't good enough to become a judge. Judges aren't kids that grow up in trailers on their racist great grandfather's land. I wasn't good enough for that.

There are a few places in the US where you don't have to be a lawyer to be a judge like Missouri. In the rest of the United States, we have legal decisions that are important and are of consequence, so they don't just let some asshole with zero legal training throw on a black robe and walk into a courtroom. Even if I went to Missouri with my legal training and practical experience, I would doubt myself. I'd still say that I wasn't good enough. To me, there's a stink of mediocrity that could never be covered up, no matter how many achievements I knock out.

The judge welcomes everyone and walks the potential jurors through what is going to happen at the trial. She is reading from a book that all judges are given that explains all of the legal principles and I can already feel some of the people start to zone out in the room. Hell, even my thoughts were starting to drift away. Whoever wrote that part was so fucking boring. Come on man, make it a bit interesting! No one wants to be on jury duty. Someone should put some serious thought into making a video with cartoons that explains the whole process. I learned more about government from that Schoolhouse Rock video "I'm Just a Bill" than I did of four years studying political science. Some people are visual learners and other people can't go 7 seconds without playing with their phone. As I'm convincing myself that this is a fantastic idea, I became aware that I'm still shuffling through these papers for some reason. Ass sweat at 75%.

The judge explains that the clerk is going to pick out 14 names, 12 potential jurors and 2 alternates. Then what's going to happen is that the prosecutor and I are going to be able to ask them questions to see if they'd be a good fit for the jury. Jury duty is basically an interview in front of a bunch of strangers for a job that no one wants. However, it does pay you 12 bucks a day, so there's that. They pay you in a check so you have to waste time signing it and trying to electronically deposit it on your phone so after factoring in all the time fucking around with it, you make about $2.37. Oh, how could I forget? They also pay you 50 cents per mile you get for travel to the courthouse. In no time, you're gonna be like Scrooge McDuck in the introduction to Duck Tales, diving into a pool full of gold coins.

As the judge is explaining the process, I think about how the justice system has duped us all. It's called jury duty. They picked the word duty. A duty is an obligation. If duty is involved it sounds like you're not going to get paid much at all to fulfill that duty. You're going to get 12 bucks a day and a bologna sandwich to sit in a courthouse and try and stay awake. Doctors have the Hippocratic Oath to do no harm. That sounds like a duty to me, not just an oath but those fuckers get paid all of the money and don't have to go to court. They even get out of jury duty by saying that they're a doctor. At that moment, I want to share what I've worked out with everyone in the room - how we've been bamboozled, but I don't think they'll understand it without context.

The clerk then produces this giant tumbly spinny looking thing. The kind of thing that you'd see at a bingo hall. She just pulls it out from under her desk and I chuckle to myself because it looks like there's no way that thing could have fit under there. She pulled that thing out of nowhere, like a goddamn magician. No one else got the joke because they're all too focused on their civic duty, I guess. If I'm honest, many of the people felt comfort seeing something related to bingo because there were some real old people in this jury pool. We didn't have to worry about their cell phones going off during the trial because they probably left their Jitterbugs in their Buicks out in the parking lot. It's weird that the older people get the more likely they're going to be called for jury duty. I think the older you get the less you should be bothered for things like that. If you want to show up, okay, but I don't want you to have to be on a jury over 65 if you don't want to. You've suffered enough civic duty and obligation. Just stay at home and do a puzzle or something. At that moment, I would have loved to be at home with my gout foot propped up watching "The Big Lebowski" for the 88th time.

The clerk spins the tumbler thing around and pulls out the first name. She reads it out loud in that dull and listless way that people read off names. It's tense for a moment until the man whose name was called groaned. I chuckle and crack a smile. I mark his name down on this oversized sheet of paper that the court gives the lawyer when the trial starts. The size is four times the size of a placemat you get at Denny's. You use it to mark down the names of the jurors, the time that the jury was sworn in and when opening arguments started. It's like jury bingo, a score card for a jury trial. I never know what I do with them after the trial. I regret not saving this one.

I shuffle through the pile of juror questionnaires and find his name. A few days before trial, I meticulously reviewed all of the juror questionnaires. I wanted to see who might be a good juror for us and who'd be a bad juror for us. Most of these old white people were gonna be bad jurors for us. Most of the people said that they knew or had a relative that was in law enforcement. They seemed like the group of people that would watch George Floyd being murdered and say "he should have stopped resisting." While it's not nice to judge people without knowing them, that's what jury selection is. I have to put people into categories. Old and white? Yeah, probably not going to be sympathetic to a young black guy even if I'd dressed him like a white guy. These people don't seem overtly prejudiced, they're from the Midwest. They'd wait to voice their prejudices when they get home. There's maybe one Hispanic person in the entire jury pool. He was the only brown person. He may not even have been Hispanic. It's not like I could ask him that. "Where's your family from, amigo? Objection. Dammit!" My job went from trying to find good jurors for us to trying to get rid of who'd be really bad for us.

Jury selection is one of my favorite parts of the trial. For those of you lucky or unlucky enough to have served on a jury before you're familiar with the process. If you haven't served on a jury before, it's where the lawyers get to ask you questions to find out

119

whether you'd be a good person on the jury. It's called *voir dire*.
It's French. Don't ask me why we use French talk in our American
legal system, dammit! It translates "to speak the truth." It's ironic
to me because potential jurors never answer these questions
honestly. Some lawyers really prepare a list of questions to ask
every person and they stick to that list. It's incredibly boring to
watch. I write out the traits of the perfect juror in my case and then
ask questions to see if the person sitting in the jury box would be a
fit with those qualifications. I don't know if that's what you're
supposed to do, but that's what I do. It's an important part of the
trial because It's the first time that the jury gets to hear the lawyers
speak. Well, there is a bit right before they swear all of the people
in the jury pool in and give them an oath where they have the
lawyers introduce themselves but it's nothing more than "Hi, my
name is Nick Leydorf. I'm here representing Mr. Defendant who is
definitely not a murderer. Thank you."

Jury selection is only fun for the lawyers. For the 95% of
potential jurors, it seems like they'd rather get anally probed than
answer questions in public in front of a group of strangers. There's
a range of emotions from jurors. It's anywhere between acting
thoroughly confused (maybe it's because they haven't taken their
pills yet) and being pissed off. It always makes me chuckle. As I
enjoyed myself a bit, my ass sweat concentration levels dropped,
it's now down to 72%.

I work my way through the people in the jury box, asking my
questions. I'm trying to get a read on these people. It's something
that I think I'm fairly good at but who knows, I could make up my
mind about the wrong person. "Juror Number 3, how do you feel
about the English rock band, Oasis? What's Oasis? Alright, get
him outta here."

Lawyers are able to remove a potential juror for two reasons.
The first is for cause, which is like if some old lady stood up and
said "I hate black people and there's no way you could convince
me otherwise." That's a pretty good reason to get rid of ol' whitey.

120

In this jury, there was a lady whom I didn't know that said she knew my mom and my family. She said that it was something that she'd be thinking about throughout the trial and it could probably affect her decision making. The judge, prosecutor and I agreed that we should excuse her for cause. I don't know if what she said was true, but if it wasn't it was a real brilliant move to make up some bullshit to get off of having to serve on a jury trial that was scheduled to take 3 weeks.

When the judge said that the trial was going to take 3 weeks, you could have heard a pin drop. Everyone wanted to mention that they had children, a job, book club or a scrabble habit in order to try and get off of this jury. But the judge wasn't having it. Remember the duty part of jury duty?

The second way a lawyer can get a potential juror excused is through a preemptory challenge. You don't have to give a reason for that. You can just say "I'd like to thank and excuse Juror number 12, your honor" and that's it. They're done. To me, it's like the golden ticket if I was a juror. "I'm out baby, I'm out!" I had one lady in a trial mean mug me after I used a peremptory challenge on her in an assault trial. My client was also black and her name was Dorothy. Again, I was totally prejudging her, but I think I stand on pretty solid ground with an assumption that someone named Dorothy doesn't trust black people. The only old white woman named Dorothy that I'd trust on that jury was the one from Golden Girls. The preemptory challenge must be a challenge for the potential juror with anxiety. "Why did they get rid of me?" I'll never tell, muhahaha!

Once things get moving with jury selection, my ass sweat percentage continues to decrease. 72, 71, and before long we were down into the high 60%s. At least I didn't notice it that much. I had my back to the gallery of potential jurors and I didn't notice anyone snickering like "Hey look, the bald lawyer has a sweaty ass!" or anything like that.

Throughout this process, I'm checking in with my client to see who he has good feelings about and who he has bad feelings about. I remember him leaning in to me and saying with some real stank ass jail breath "I don't have a good feelings about any of these motherfuckers." After we weren't on the same page with clothing style, it's nice to see there's one thing that he and I could agree on.

What I gathered from the prosecutor's strategy was that he wanted to keep anyone on the jury that had anyone who had relatives in law enforcement. He had a plethora of these folks to choose from. He used a preemptory on a young woman that I had targeted as my best potential juror. The answer to one of my questions about law enforcement was basically "Fuck the police." I wanted to yell "NO! Come on!" It did seem unfair, especially considering that there were no black people in the pool of potential jurors. Just let me have this one, dammit!

I was able to whittle my way through the really bad potential jurors. One dude had a Toby Keith t-shirt on. In the immortal words of Randy Jackson "Yeah, it's a no for me dawg." Next. However, like the folksy words of a Travis Tritt song, there comes a point where you have to just live with what you have. My son, Julian, who's 9, would say "You get what you get, and you don't throw a fit." I wanted to throw a fit. I tried to find people with some critical thinking skills. It was slim pickin's here. I always like people that are nurses or teachers. They deal with all kinds of humans everyday. They have a way of being able to cut through all of the bullshit. As I used my last preemptory challenge, I felt good about the work I'd done. I also wished I had about 30 more preemptory challenges. All told, it took about two and a half hours for the prosecutor and I to pick the jury.

After the prosecutor and I told the judge that we were satisfied with the jury, the potential jurors who didn't get picked simultaneously exhaled a big sigh of relief. We took a break. As I was walking out of the courtroom, an older gentleman said to me "Good luck. It sounds like you're going to have your work cut out for you on this one." I laughed and said "thanks." I wanted to mouth the words "take me with you," but there was no time. I needed to take another shit before we started back up again.

Why I Hate Being A Lawyer

Before we get into this, I understand that there are good things about being a lawyer. However, when things like what I'm going to describe to you happen, the good things get thrown out the window. In 2020, during the height of COVID-19, I fired a client because he was an asshole. Then he tried to get into my office even though he was told several times to never come back.

Earlier that morning, I appeared on Zoom in court (I put pants on for this one) and told the judge that there had been a breakdown of the attorney-client relationship. Whenever you hear a lawyer say, "Judge, there was a breakdown of the attorney-client relationship," it means "this person is an asshole and I can't deal with them anymore." At 40, I don't like being told what to do. The interaction with this client was a huge moment for me, standing up for myself.

He hired me to represent him for a drunk driving. It was his third offense. In my opinion, if you get one drunk driving it's not a big deal. People make mistakes. I get that. If you do it once, you should learn how dangerous it is to get behind the wheel and never do it again. However, not everyone learns the first time. If you get another one I'm like "dude, you gotta figure this out." If you get arrested for a third one, you have a fucking problem. Let's call this guy Larry. Larry called me and we talked on the phone and met on Zoom. I never met him in person before I agreed to take his case. I will never make that mistake again. There are things that you learn from being in the same room that you'll never learn from them in a Zoom meeting. Like whether they're a fucking crazy person.

Larry was arrested toward the end of 2019. However, because there was a search warrant for his blood to be drawn, he wasn't charged by the prosecuting attorney until 2020. That meant that Larry needed to turn himself in to be arraigned on the charge of Operating While Intoxicated - 3rd Offense, aka Boozin' and Cruisin' x3. Even though there was a pandemic going on, certain courts and jails were still requiring people to come into be arraigned. If I haven't explained this already, an arraignment is where they formally read the charge to you and ask what your plea is, guilty or not guilty.

To me, making people physically come into a jail during a pandemic is as stupid as it gets. We're trying to stop the spread of COVID-19 so let's keep people out of jail as best as we can, let's not encourage them to get together. At that time, the Lansing City Jail had no procedures to test whether someone had COVID-19 symptoms like a fever either. Someone could have the fucking thing and then come in and spread it to everyone in the jail. It doesn't take a fucking brain surgeon to figure out that's a bad idea. However, people tend to not give a shit about people they consider to be criminals. If this was your grandma, you would give a shit but because this is someone who's accused of committing a crime it's easy to say "well, you shouldn't have committed a crime."

He and I schedule a time where he's going to turn himself into the jail and I will then appear by Zoom for his arraignment. This is what I was told would happen by the court. It seems weird to me because if they have to be there in person, then I think that I should have to be there in person too. There have been times during COVID where a required my client to be present for sentencing and said I could appear by Zoom and I declined. I wanted to be there with them. It's scary enough and not being there when there was an option to be physically present seemed like the wrong thing to do. Also, if they're going to say some shit to the judge, I want to be able to stomp on their foot or jab 'em in the ribs to get them to stop talking. I can't do that if I'm on Zoom. However, the court didn't give me that option, I had to appear by Zoom and Larry had to be there in person.

I knew from the beginning that Larry had a lot of anxiety because he told me when we spoke on the phone and during the Zoom meeting when he hired me. I could also tell because I have a lot of anxiety too, so game recognizes game, or whatever that saying is. Unfortunately, I had no idea of what I would be working with when I took on Larry's case.

When we schedule the time for Larry to turn himself in, I gave him the address and told him that he had to be there no later than 9am. The court told me that if Larry wasn't there before 9am that morning, then they would hold Larry in jail until the next morning when the court did arraignments again. I relayed all of this info to Larry and made sure that he understood that he was going to have to be there before 9am. Larry and I agreed that he would be there at 845am at the latest. I felt confident that he understood that he needed to be there at that time or earlier because those words came out of his mouth and I heard them with the sound holes on each side of my head.

The rest of the week went by and I didn't hear anything from him. I told him that this was going to be the beginning of the entire criminal process and that if he had questions, he should call me before the weekend because he was going to turn himself in on Monday morning. At what time? That's right, no later than 9am. I'm glad you're paying attention. The rest of the week blows by and I don't think anything of it.

I wake up Monday morning and walk out into the kitchen and make coffee like I do every morning. I pour 12 cups of water up to the line in the carafe and then pour a liberal amount of 8 O'Clock medium roast coffee into the pot. Then I scratch my ass and go downstairs to take a shower. I look at my phone and I have a missed call and 3 text messages from Larry, all from 6am. I'm like "what the fuck?" He wants to know where is he supposed to go and what time was he supposed to be there. Was it 6am or 9am? In the distance, a dude raises one red flag. Seriously, Larry? You call me at 6am thinking you're supposed to be in court at 6am? What fucking court is open at 6am? I've heard of Night Court but never watched it on TV. This isn't night court, this is regular fucking day court, fam. Don't fucking blow up my phone at 6am on a Monday morning when I walked your ass through EXACTLY what you were going to be doing.

Rather than call him at this early hour, I wasn't even wearing pants, I decided to text him. I tell him no, it's before 9am and then I take a screenshot of exactly where he is supposed to go, you know, the place that I told his ass to be when we talked on the phone and he knew right where it was.

He then calls me but I missed it because 1) it was like 6:15 in the morning and 2) I was washing my face and butt in the shower. I get out of the shower and there are more calls and text messages from Larry. Not sure what these are but it's 6:15 so I decide to put clothes on my clean and naked body and I'll call Larry on the way to the office.

I get in my car and call him. Larry picks up and he's breathing heavy like he's just been running. He tells me that this isn't going to work if I don't answer his questions immediately. Mother fucker, it's 6am in the mother fucking morning. This wasn't like I threw all of this information on you, I talked with your dumb ass and we went over every detail because his dumb ass said "I want to go over every detail." Red flag #2 rises in the distance.

I get a bit snarky with Larry on the phone because I don't handle stupidity well. I've found that stupid people are a complete waste of my time. As a criminal defense attorney, I'm told what to do on a regular basis. Courts are like "Be here on Friday at

8:30am. What, you have something else going on? Guess what? We don't give a shit." I don't have much free time so I don't want some idiot wasting my time. The only person that I want wasting my time is myself.

When I deploy the snark on Larry, he immediately comes back with attitude. He says that he has anxiety and doesn't need his lawyer "popping off" at him. Bro, if anyone has popped off, its the dude that's giving me attitude on the phone at 6:45am. Also, I have anxiety too. I've had anxiety since way back in the goddamn George W. Bush presidency. Don't talk to me about mother fucking anxiety. I'm an OG when it comes to anxiety.

However, I want you to understand that while I'm writing this from the perspective of the confident attorney that has had time to reflect on ol' Larry, at the time I handled things completely differently. Being a lawyer transformed me into a gigantic pussy. Why? Because I'm constantly afraid of being disciplined by the bar association or having someone leave me a negative review. That's no way to live. It's like being emotionally neutered. I can't feel and react like a human being because if I do, someone is going to file a grievance against my law license or they're going to leave me a 1 star review on Google. I should be able to react without fear of those things. If someone off the street tried to treat me like shit, I would just tell them they're an asshole and that they should, in fact, go fuck themselves. However, because I'm a lawyer I can't, or at least I don't believe that I can.

Larry loses his shit on the phone. He calls me all kinds of names. He says I'm a shitty lawyer. At the time, I try and talk him through this, but it's not working. He hangs the phone up on me. That's 3 red flags. I should have said "okay, that's it, I'm out," but I didn't. Anytime anyone hangs up the phone on me, I become enraged. It's probably because I wanted to hang up on them but I feel I can't because I'm a lawyer and I have to be all professional or whatever. I call Larry back and tell him that he needs to calm down and we need to get this warrant taken care of this morning.

128

Somehow he shifts instantly from being a raging lunatic to "okay, I'll go do this now, bye." I'm on the side of the road in my KIA thinking "how the fuck did I get to this point in my life?"

I drive to the office and contact the court and let them know that he turned himself in at the jail. They give me the Zoom info for the hearing that was going to take place later that morning. I was in shock and shut down. There's a thing that really fucked up people do which is called gaslighting. It's where they try and flip the script in such a way that they try and normalize their behavior and make you feel like you're the one that was wrong. It's really messed up. Turns out that in addition being arrested for drunk driving, Larry had a Ph. D in gaslighting. I sat alone in my office the entire morning considering whether I was the bad guy in this situation.

Had I wronged him? Oh no, I'm the bad person here. It was such a confusing place to be in. When you're dealing with offenders in the criminal justice system, there's a higher rate of these types of people than if you were to be a plumber. Criminal defendants often have a way of shifting the cause of their problems to other people rather than themselves. It's easier to deal with the fact that you murdered someone if you feel you were justified in doing so rather than you're a monster. It's easy to attack your lawyer because that's the person that you are in contact the most in the criminal justice system and guess what? They aren't allowed to talk about your bullshit with anyone! You can treat them like shit, and no one is the wiser. Upon reflection, I'm writing this because I've had enough of the way that this system is set up. For the guy that threatened to kill me, I'm going to talk about that shit. For Larry, you were a dick and I'm going to talk about it. I shouldn't have to keep all of that inside and end up dying at 53 years old from throat cancer because I didn't speak the truth.

After Larry's next-level tantrum happened, the I wasn't able to process what had happened because I had a job to do. I should have cut ties immediately with Larry. My insecurities about money caused me to believe that if I gave Larry back his money, the sheriff was going to be at our house evicting us because we didn't have enough money to pay the rent. Nothing could have been further from the truth, but that's how my alligator brain functions when I am overtaken with anxiety. If I have to give him his money back, then I'm not going to have any money. I'm not rich, but I'm not poor either. I'm not as far along as I would like to be as far as retirement. The $800 monthly student loan payment doesn't help with that either. My point is that my fear and insecurities caused me to conclude that I was going to be homeless if I didn't take on this guy's case. It was a scenario that my brain came up with because it thought it had to save me from danger. However, that danger never existed at all. I'm thankful for that part of my brain that looks out to protect me. If I can learn how to use it for good, then there's nothing that can stop me. It doesn't help that I'm a creative person, so that really ramps up the worst-case scenarios. Oh no, if you don't take this case, then you're going to be evicted from your home immediately. Then you're going to have to blow a dude for crank behind the Quality Dairy over on Michigan Avenue while another homeless guy plays "Careless Whisper" on the Tenor Sax.

Enough about me for a moment. Let's talk about Larry. I wanted nothing more than to tell him to fuck off, but I didn't. When I first met him on Zoom, he presented as a genuinely nice person. He greeted me with a nice "how are you doing this morning?" He had long scraggly hair, a thin face, and a slight mustache. He presented like a young hipster Jesus. He also said "God bless" a lot. He also answered when I asked him how his day was with "Oh, I'm blessed." Now I've come to know that all of that was total bullshit. It was just a mask to cover up the bubbling rage that he tried, mostly unsuccessfully, to keep below the surface. It was like Larry wanted to look like Jesus because he felt the whole world was against him. He was the victim. His problems were the product of the world crucifying him. That's the mindset of most criminals. I think it's referred to as an external locus of control. When I fuck up, I look inward to figure out what the cause was. With other folks like Larry, they tend to look outward for an explanation for their fuck ups. While I would say that if I were late for a meeting because I forgot to set an alarm.

People like Larry would say that someone else made them late. It's a coping mechanism. One that makes it easier to deal with their own inadequacies. It's much simpler to blame one's problems on what other people did to us rather than taking personal responsibility for our actions. The Jesus get-up may have been a coincidence, but it seemed to line up with how I psychoanalyzed Larry. I may be wrong, but I'm probably not. I've had the privilege to deal with a great number of assholes since I started practicing law. I'm not going to blame anyone else for that. This was my choice. The goal is to learn from this and move on to make sure that I don't put myself in positions like this in the future, so I don't have to deal with the Larrys of the world.

His Zoom arraignment went off without a hitch. The magistrate called me to let me know that the hearing would be starting. I logged in, and there were no problems whatsoever. Larry was able to use his Jesus-y facade to charm the magistrate, even from the jail cell in the city lockup. The magistrate had no idea that hours earlier, Larry had had a fucking meltdown and was screaming at me on the phone using words that would make his lord and savior upset.

After the arraignment, I called his girlfriend to let her know what had happened. She was thankful and apologetic for Larry's behavior. I did something that I normally wouldn't do. I asked her whether this was something that had happened often. Mrs. Larry said that she knew he had anxiety, but that they hadn't been together long and had never seen him act like that before. Damn, girl. You better see your future. I am only dealing with Larry for a few months, and he's paying me. You're in this for the long haul, and you're not getting paid to deal with Larry's tantrums. In a very lawyerly way, I suggested that she have him look into seeing someone to talk about his anxiety. If this was how he was dealing with this and the case was just starting, things were not going to be getting any easier. I said this for her benefit, but I should have been listening to what I was telling her because this wasn't the first time that I was going to have to deal with Larry's child-like tendencies.

After Larry was released, he sent me a few text messages. As I would learn, Larry was of the school that instead of sending one text message, four are sent. It seems like a passive-aggressive way of saying, "hey, listen to me." Getting four messages in a minute is looked at in our society as being a non-issue, but to me, it's aggressive. What was odd about Larry's messages was that he attributed his meltdown to miscommunication on both of our parts. Yikes, bro. There was no miscommunication on my part at all. I was merely a trash can that you were trying to dump all of your garbage in. There's no miscommunication when you call me up and scream on the phone at me and tell me I'm a shitty lawyer when you're a 30-something man, and you can't deal with your emotions. That's not miscommunication; that's mental illness. Instead of saying that was a miscommunication, you should take my advice to talk to someone. When I suggested that to Larry, he told me he didn't want to take any pills for his anxiety. First, I didn't say anything about taking any pills; I just want you to talk to somebody about this. Larry also runs a business, and this kind of rage is like a bomb that could go off at any second. No pills had to be involved in a conversation to talk about how you've reached the point to think that treating another human being the way you did is acceptable for you.

Then how is it that you're able to change the facts to fit the conclusion that this wasn't you, it was something that someone did that happened to you? I was the lawyer. I was the one that had not given him the details, and I should have known that he had anxiety, so I had to give him a bit of grace and understanding. Bullshit. He's the one with the undiagnosed mental condition that he's refused to look at. Things happen to us, and it's our choice to see what we do with the aftermath. You can take the opportunity to learn and grow or you can use it as a crutch. I'm saying this for myself as much as I'm saying it for people like Larry. There's no justification or excuse for why he acted the way he did. There's an explanation, which is that he has bad anxiety. That doesn't justify him treating other people like pieces of shit, and then blaming them for it. Now that's over, it was up to me to deal with it.

I started putting up boundaries with how I was going to deal with Larry. Rather than getting rid of him altogether as a client, which is what I should have done, I decided that I would remain calm in all of my interactions with him. I'll be straightforward and matter-of-fact with Larry. I can only control my reactions to people. I can't control what other people are going to do. Easier said than done.

A month or so went by after Larry's meltdown. The case was on hold because it had been moved out to give me more time to get all of the police reports and video evidence from the traffic stop that ended with Larry's arrest. Here's the thing - Larry had a good case. Normally, drunk driving arrests are complete shit shows. Someone gets pulled over for swerving all over the road, they admit to drinking, they go through the field sobriety tests on the side of the road (I like to call them the Drunk Olympics), and they blow into the portable breathalyzer test. They blow two times the legal limit, and they're arrested and go to jail. There's crying, begging, and bargaining with the officer to just let them go.

Larry's case had nothing like that. He was pulled over by an officer, who was young enough to be my son, for having a headlight out. There was no bad driving. Larry's blood work came back at .08, the lowest amount of alcohol you can have in your blood and still be arrested for drunk driving. I was going to have several arguments that I could make to try and get this case dismissed or plea bargain way down to something that wouldn't put Larry in a pickle.

This kind of case is a dream for criminal defense lawyers. We usually have to deal with cases that have bad facts. We look forward to the cases like this where we can fight for our clients. This would have been a great case for me, except the client was Larry. If I haven't said it before, Larry turned out to be a giant fucking asshole.

After I had a chance to review all of the videos and reports, I reached out to the prosecutor again. She already hadn't responded to my three emails about the file. I was curious to find out how she was going to get around the bad facts for her in this case. That's the thing about prosecutors, they can be lazy. I get that they have job security because a lot of prosecutors don't return phone calls or emails, but come on. We're dealing with other people's lives here, and also just fucking pick up the phone and get back with me out of professional courtesy. We're both lawyers. We both have jobs to do. If you don't want to return phone calls, then go become a Sandwich Artist at Subway. It gets on my nerves when prosecutors don't return phone calls because they put things off until the last minute and expect you to get back with them immediately because they've waited until the last minute to get off their asses and do something. She didn't respond to my fourth email and that shouldn't have surprised me. I've dealt with her before, and she's a real pile of garbage. I made some calls to other people and learned that their office had rotated prosecutors to different assignments. Now the pile of garbage prosecutor wasn't on the case any longer. Larry's case had a new prosecutor handling the file.

I emailed this new prosecutor, and he got back to me immediately. He was young and had no clue what I was talking about because he was so new, but it was refreshing to talk with someone about this case on the phone. He said that he was going to have to talk with his supervisor about this case and he'd get back to me. Yeah, I'm sure you will, junior. We'll talk in a month after I send five emails and leave three voicemails.

To my surprise, he called me back later that afternoon. I was like, "holy shit, this guy seems like a normal person that I can reason with. How refreshing!" He makes my client a plea offer to dismiss the felony if he pleads to a misdemeanor offense. It wasn't what I was looking for, but it was better than the offer that the first prosecutor emailed me, probably while she was taking a dump. I told Prosecutor #2 that I would talk this over with my client and get back to him. I thought the time between my client's initial tantrum and now would have given him some perspective and how he needed to get his shit together. Haha! Oh, Nick, that's cute.

I don't want it to sound like I don't care about his anxiety or anyone else's mental condition. What I don't care for is when someone knows that they have something like this and refuses to seek any help or treatment. Screaming at your attorney on the phone when you're the one that fucked up the date and time is completely inappropriate. There's no way I can give you a free pass for that. I can empathize with people that have mental conditions. I have dealt with numerous people over the past 18 years who have had mental conditions, both diagnosed and undiagnosed. It isn't fair that people have these conditions. However, it's up to them to do something about it. You can't use things like mental conditions to get out of situations where you are clearly in the wrong. Otherwise, the concept of personal responsibility doesn't work anymore. You can say, "Oh, I'm sorry, this is why this happened. It doesn't excuse the fact that I was a douchebag, but I think it might help explain why it happened." That may sound like semantics, but to me, it's the difference between giving someone a free pass and holding them accountable for their behavior.

I called up Larry right after I got off the phone with Prosecutor #2. I asked Larry how he was doing, and he said, "Blessed as always." Yuck, not a good start to the conversation. That fake religious bullshit gets under my skin, especially when it comes out of the mouth of a phony baloney kind of person. After my eyeballs returned from their trip to the back of my head, I moved past it and told Larry that I had a conversation with the prosecutor and needed to talk with him about it. I started by explaining why there had been a delay in getting some additional information on his case - I was dealing with a lazy-ass prosecutor, but she finally got reassigned. Before I could go any further, Larry started complaining about how it had been some time since he'd heard from me. Yeah, dipshit, I was explaining that. I also explained that to him in a text message a week before, and he responded with "thank you for the update and God bless." We weren't off to a great start. I made sure that before this call, I grounded myself. It's something that my wife has taught me how to do when I'm going to go into stressful situations. So much for grounding myself here. Larry had already interrupted me once and was complaining about how I hadn't been holding his hand.

After Larry finished his initial pre-prepared spiel about how he hadn't heard anything from me, I tried to get him back on course by saying that I had an offer that the prosecutor made that I had to talk with him about and get his input. I shared with him where things were at and reminded him what their first offer had been, which was basically nothing. Then I explained to Larry what this offer was. The felony charge would be dismissed and he would enter a plea of guilty to a misdemeanor offense of drunk driving.

Larry interpreted me calling him and telling him what the terms of a new plea offer were with me trying to make him give me an answer on the spot. He started to get irritated with me and said that I wasn't working for him. To Larry, I was working for the prosecutor. Obviously, that's absurd. He kept pushing and interrupting me. I finally stepped out of lawyer mode and into the mode that I envision a kindergarten teacher acting like to get one of their students to calm down after they dropped their lunch tray on the floor. "Ok, Larry, let's take a deep breath." However, Larry wasn't able to calm down. He interpreted the delay in the prosecutor getting back to me as the prosecutor being out to get him and that he wasn't going to cooperate no matter what. At that point, I hadn't been able to explain to Larry that he had an option to reject the plea offer altogether. I was trying to get him to listen, but it wasn't working. I told Larry that it was my job to discuss all plea offers made by the prosecution. I wasn't making any recommendations at that point because I hadn't even been able to get 50 words out of my mouth. I was having to deal with this most recent freak-out from Larry. I was just trying to do my job, the one that Larry paid me to do, and I wasn't able to do it because of classic Larry behavior.

Larry continued to get more heated. He accused me of not helping him. He then told me to "back the fuck off." Larry said that he wasn't going to give me an answer at that moment about the plea agreement. I said that was fine, and I didn't expect him to. However, I wanted to discuss this with him when he calmed down. What set him off was that I said I could probably get him more time to think about things, but the prosecutor would need to agree to that because we had court coming up. Then Larry goes off saying that I care more about the prosecutor than I care about him. Now Larry's angry and he's yelling again at me. He says he's ending the call and then hangs up the phone.

I'm livid. Again. All I am trying to do is help this asshole, and Larry isn't letting me. A huge part of my job is being able to communicate with my client. If I can't communicate with my client, I can't do my job. I felt a sickness building inside me. All I wanted to do was have a conversation with Larry to talk about his case and, again, his attitude wouldn't allow for it. He was not allowing me to do my job, and he's accusing me of working with the other side against him. This was some real tin-foil hat type of shit, and I didn't want any part of it.

These complaints made me feel worthless, like I was one of those shitty attorneys that you hear about screwing over one of their clients. Constantly gas-lighting myself eroded my sense of identity. I didn't have the confidence to know that I have worth and did not deserve to be spoken to or treated like that. Even though I may have exuded that outwardly, it was in those quiet moments I was constantly questioning myself.

I sat alone in my office and took a few minutes to consider what I should do. This, on top of what happened a month ago, was yet another red flag that I needed to get out of this case. I talked with other Nick about the situation and what happened before his arraignment. He agreed that I should file a motion to withdraw as his attorney.

I went back to my office, and the sickness inside my gut was accented by the frustration and anger following my conversation with Larry. Again, I felt like my career put me in a straight jacket. If Larry and his skinny Jesus-lookin' ass pulled this kind of shit on me in real life, I would tell him to go fuck off. However, if I told a client to go fuck off, there's a chance that they would call the bar association and file a grievance against my license. I know a lawyer that used shit on the phone with a client, and the client reported them to the bar association. I didn't want to deal with that. So I just sat there and took it. I felt emasculated. I felt like he had all the control in the situation, and my only recourse was to ask the court to let me out of the case. It seemed like the goodie-two-shoes approach, but that's all I had. I could either put up with Larry's bullshit, or I could get out of the case.

I decided that my mental health was more important than the money. Larry paid me a flat fee for the case. That meant that I would have to calculate how much time I had into the case and refund the balance to him. Other than a kick to the dick, I didn't want to have to give Larry back anything. Fuck Larry. He treated me like shit when I was the only one that was fighting for him, and now I have to give money back to him? Fuck that. However, if I wanted to keep being a lawyer, something I keep reevaluating every day, then I have to play by those rules.

I called the court and spoke with the clerk. I told her that I would like the court to hear my motion to withdraw as counsel for

Larry that Friday morning. I would draft the motion and submit it to the court. The clerk gave me the Zoom room information. I hung up and started drafting my motion to withdraw.

You might be thinking that I put everything that happened with Larry in my motion to withdraw. However, an attorney can't do that. Ethics require that those conversations remain subject to the attorney-client relationship. I had to be vague in my motion to the court. I said there had been a breakdown in the attorney-client relationship with Larry, but I didn't say specifically why. I really wanted to tell this judge how much of an asshole Larry was, but again, I wasn't able to be a human being. So much of being a defense attorney is being a fucking law robot. Someone can tell you that they killed someone, and you can't tell anyone about that. You're just supposed to sit with that inside of you. That's something that a robot can do very easily because they don't have emotions yet. But that's difficult shit for a human being to keep inside them.

I was vague in my motion and said that Larry needed to find another lawyer. That was about it. I sent it to the court, and the prosecutor and I started writing an email to Larry.

In my email to Larry, I was more direct and less formal. I let him know that his behavior prevented me from doing my job again. I didn't want to get into specific details with him however I wanted to let him know that how he has treated me for the second time now was not okay. I told him that I understand that he has anxiety because I too have anxiety; however, that's not an excuse to take out his frustration on me. I told him it's not part of my job to be his punching bag. I closed the email by attaching the motion to withdraw as his lawyer and gave him the Zoom room information for Friday.

As I was writing this, I received another four text messages from Larry. He blamed me for caring about the prosecutor's time and that he felt like I was telling him that he was wasting everyone's time by not giving me an immediate decision. With each text message that came in, the decision that I had made to fire him as a client was seeming like the correct one.

I hit send on the email, knowing that it wouldn't be the last time that I heard from Larry. Sure enough, six minutes later he calls me. I don't know why I answered. Actually, I know why I answered. I was giving myself another chance to tell Larry what a piece of shit he was. Fortunately or unfortunately, depending on the way you look at me continuing to be a lawyer, I didn't tell Larry what I thought of him. Larry asked me whether I filed the motion to withdraw with the court. "Uh, yeah, that's what I said in the email." I reiterated that I had no responsibility to continue to work with someone that acted like this. He told me, "you're not the victim here." When I heard that, it made me pause for a moment. This is the kind of gaslighting bullshit that people pull to get you to sympathize with them. It turned out that in addition to being a drunk driver on two occasions, Larry was also a master manipulator. However, nice try, Larry, I wasn't falling for this bullshit. Yes, I am the victim here because I don't deserve to be treated like shit, asshole. Get your fucking shit together because there's no way another lawyer or a judge is going to put up with your behavior. In an unexpected plot twist, Larry went from I was a shitty lawyer to can we work this out? It was exhausting, and at the end of the conversation (I say conversation because I only said like three words), I was spent. All told, it took me over three hours to clean up the mess that Larry caused that afternoon. Remember how it all started? I wanted to have a conversation with Larry, and his dumb ass misinterpreted this as me telling him what to do.

The next few days went along without any Larry in my life. It was nice. Then like it does every week, Friday morning came. It was the day of the hearing before the judge on my motion to withdraw as his attorney. I assumed that I would just see Larry on Zoom, but alas, I underestimated the power of Larry.

About a half hour before the hearing, Larry calls. Learning from my mistakes, I don't answer. Larry left a message with my answering service that I had given him the wrong Zoom room information. Sometimes I know I can make mistakes with things like that because on occasion, I tendency to rush, like when I am trying to end telephone conversations with dickheads. However, I knew that on this occasion, I had given Larry the correct information because I didn't want his crazy ass to call me saying that I had given him the wrong information. So I decided to be very detached emotionally. I opened the email that I had sent Larry and copied and pasted the room information. I then joined the room to test it out, and holy shit, I had given him the correct information. Wowsers!

I sent Larry a text because I had no desire to speak with him at all. I said the room information was correct, and I copied and pasted the sentence from my email to him. I said "No, check the email again." In my way, this was the first step to taking back my power in this, or at least I would think it was. I think this was just an incredibly sad attempt by Larry to try and strike up a conversation with me prior to the hearing. He probably figured out that he was the one in the wrong and wanted to see if I would continue to represent him. Saying that I had given him the wrong information wasn't the right way to do it, but I don't expect much from a person like Larry.

Larry then fires off four texts in quick succession. He wants to know if I had "time to cool off and think about this?" What the fuck?! Cool off?! Despite the exclamation points in the previous sentences, I'm not the one that needed to cool off. Larry's was the one that needed to cool off. I should have been sending him that text. After two times of seeing red with me when all I was trying to do was do my job, he had the fucking stones to say, "Had time to cool off, bud?" OOOOF! I felt like I was getting Punk'd. Where's Ashton? This shit cannot be real. This buffoon did not just text did you have time to cool off to me! Again, I shifted into Lawyer Budda mode and chose not to respond and give him my energy at the time. But I want you to know that inside I was angry. Going

141

back one level I think I was also scared. I just wanted this person out of my life. It wasn't a Love Connection and I wanted the show to end. I continued to ignore the messages from this morning and waited for the hearing to start. Namaste, motherfucker.

The hearing was scheduled for 8:30 am on a Friday morning. I logged into the room at about 8:25, expecting that I would have a little bit of a wait. I did not. The Zoom hearing room connected immediately, and I joined a hearing room where the judge and Prosecutor #2 were both in the courtroom. Larry's dumb face was also there. Larry motioned to someone off-camera, and his girlfriend entered the frame. Awesome. Maybe she'd inject a bit of sanity into this hearing? I had talked with her the day of the arraignment, where Larry had his first tantrum, and she seemed normal. At the time, she seemed receptive to my idea that Larry should employ a brain-wrangler to wrestle those demons bouncing around his ol' noggin.

I was feeling awkward and nervous. More so than usual. I was breaking up with a client, and instead of getting to do it on our own time, I had to explain why I wanted to break up with Larry to a judge. I wasn't nervous about anything that I had done, it felt embarrassing for me to admit that there was a person that I couldn't manage even after all of these years of lawyering. I wasn't able to get him to calm down. Maybe now I'm making excuses for other crazy people's behavior? I think I may have been just going along with a lot of crazy shit over the years and had never stood up for myself. Either way, I was in uncomfortable territory.

The judge called the case and asked me about my motion to withdraw. I told her that Larry and I could no longer communicate, and I thought that it would be best that he find another lawyer. I so wanted to say to the judge what a terrible person Larry was and that he needed some immediate mental help, but those pesky rules of ethics and professional conduct rules prevented me from being a human being again. I had to be robot lawyer. Show no emotion, don't say what happened because there are rules! I don't like that feeling. I don't like being told what I have to say and what I can't say. I want to be able to get all of this out right now in this Zoom hearing. But I can't. I let the judge know that there was more to the story, but that I couldn't share it because of the attorney-client privilege. The judge should be able to read between the lines.

The judge then asked Larry what he thought of my request to be removed from his case and not to be his lawyer anymore. From the look on Larry's dumb face, it seemed as if he didn't expect that I would hold back and simply tell the judge there had been a breakdown of the attorney-client relationship. It looked as if Larry was waiting for me to launch into a blow-by-blow of all of his bullshit. You could almost see the gears turning in his stupid head. How can I manipulate this situation to benefit me? Is the look that he had on his face.

In a bold and unexpected move, Larry started with an apology to me. You read that right, gang. These words fell out of Larry's suck hole, "I want to take this opportunity to apologize to Nick," Wow, thanks, Larry. That must be hard for a person of such little personal responsibility to do. You're really growing, bud!

However, Larry's emotional awakening didn't last long because he then says that his girlfriend had listened to most of the conversations between Larry and me and she was prepared to testify. BUH-BUH-BUM!!! Oh no, his girlfriend is going to testify? What am I going to do? I should be shitting myself with fear! I wasn't. I was amazed that Larry would now lie in front of a judge. At that point, I just thought he was a shitty person. I had no idea that he was a liar. For me, you can be a shitty person, and I still might respect you. However, if you are a liar, then that bumps you way down in my book. Don't lie. Haven't you seen those after-school specials or an episode of Full House? It never pays off to lie.

Then Larry pulled a typical Larry move. He went from saying good things about you in one breath and then throwing you in front of a bus the next. The thing is, the judge had no idea what was going on. I was limited in what I could say, and Larry just apologized. Kind of. It was nice to hear the judge say after Larry offered to have his girlfriend testify, "Sir, I simply asked you if you have a problem with Mr. Leydorf withdrawing as your attorney." Yes, thank you, judge! Amen! Larry dodged the question again because he had things he wanted to say. He had paid me in full, and I didn't do the entire job for him. The logic is ridiculous. Let's say that you pay a mechanic to fix your car, and you pay him in full upfront. Don't do this, by the way, mechanics have a worse reputation than lawyers! Sorry to any mechanics that are reading this. So you pay the mechanic upfront. Then you go to the mechanic's garage to check on your car. You're not happy that he hasn't finished the job, so you call his mother a whore who used to blow burros for nickels in Tijuana. The mechanic who isn't bound by rules of ethics (nice!) tells you to go fuck yourself, and he's not working on your car anymore. You're like, "Umm, what?! I paid you to do the job, and I paid you in full." Yeah, bud, but just because you paid me to fix your car doesn't mean you could call my mother a whore.

I catch myself smiling on camera as I see Larry stumbling around with his words. His idol, Jesus, was much better at public speaking. It's hard for a gaslighter to succeed when they aren't one on one. When there are multiple people in the room, their job is exponentially more difficult, especially when one of those people is wearing a black robe and can put you in jail for contempt. I did enjoy a bit of schadenfreude watching Larry mumblin' and stumblin' his way into a hole he was digging by not answering simple questions from the judge. She asked you a simple question, bud, did you have a problem with me getting off of your case? All you had to say was either yes or no. This wasn't the time for you to become Danny DiVito in My Cousin Vinny.

After Larry tapped out because he didn't have the mental dexterity to answer a simple yes or no question, the judge went back to me and asked, "Mr. Leydorf, would you like me to put the two of you in a breakout room so you could talk?" That was a hilarious question from the judge, one that she probably didn't intend to be funny. Did you just hear this guy, judge? He's nuttier than squirrel turds. I would rather eat all of Larry's body hair than be his lawyer for one second longer. However, I learned from Larry's mistakes and answered with a simple "No." I did share that before the hearing, Larry had sent me some text messages that further supported the decision that I made to file the motion in the first place. It felt good to stand up for myself, even if I was limited in what I could say. I couldn't say, "hey, this guy's an asshole, and here's why," but I could get a bit creative and say it in another way that didn't violate the attorney-client privilege.

The judge thankfully granted my motion. I felt so relieved to be done with this guy. The judge told Larry that he would be getting a notice in the mail with his next court date and it would be on such and such a date and at such and such a time. Larry interrupts the judge and says, "Can you repeat that, I want to write this down for my records." Judges don't like to be interrupted. Judges also don't like to have to repeat themselves. I think as the face time increased between Larry and the judge, the judge could see why I didn't want to work with this guy. It was exhausting because everything from Larry was a "God bless," or some other bullshit. Dude, just shut the fuck up. Stop talking and start listening. You'd probably learn something if you quiet your mind and listen to what others have to say. But again, I was asking for too much from Larry because he wouldn't even listen to me for advice and he was paying for it.

The hearing ended and I thought I was in the clear. I felt relieved. Larry was out of my life. Now I was going to calculate my hours spent and mail him an itemized list of the time that I spent with a check for the balance that I hadn't earned yet. However, spiritually, I earned every fucking last penny of the money that Larry paid me, and then some. No one should feel as if they are in a position that they have to deal with assholes because they need the money.

I have a tremendous amount of insecurity with money. Maybe it's that I am insecure with me making the right decisions about money? As we've seen thus far, I didn't make greatest decision about my career. While I have made a decent amount of money, the degree cost me over six figures in student loans and a decade and two decades (and counting) of anxiety, so, yeah, maybe I don't trust my decision making. I felt that I had to stay on Larry's case because I needed the money. Even before that, I undercharged Larry. I have a weird complex when it comes to quoting my fee to someone. I feel like they are going to laugh at me and say that's ridiculous. It's probably because that's happened to me before. I feel as though I am not worth the fee that I quote people, even though that it is reasonable given the amount of work that would go into doing the job for them and how good I am at being a lawyer. I negotiate against myself and by the time I tell the person what the cost will be for my services, I've already cut my fee by a thousand-or-so dollars without hearing an objection from them. Maybe they would happily pay the fee that I had in mind? I'd never know it because I was too busy haggling with myself. "You're not worth it. You're going to fuck this up. You're a terrible lawyer. You should quit but you cant because you fucked up and chose this profession." That's 3% of what is going on in my head. When people like Larry come along, they reinforce those false narratives that I created. It's not fun at all. But, damn, I was glad to be rid of Larry.

Then the texts and calls started coming in from Larry. It was like the last three minutes of a public television telethon. Two calls in quick succession to my answering service. Then the text messages started. Three right off the top. Larry was angry. Maybe it was because he didn't have control in that situation and he couldn't pull the same bullshit with the judge that he did with me?

146

I didn't care. I had no desire to respond to him. Then the third call came in and I broke. I wanted to be done with this. I answered.

I said "Yes, Larry, how can I help you?" in a condescending tone. I really didn't give a shit at this point. He's not my client anymore. I'm not sure why I answered the phone. It was a combination of gloating and an injection of confidence I felt from knowing that the rest of my life would be Larry-free. Larry accused me of stealing from him. I told him that was incorrect and that I would be mailing him a check. That wasn't enough for Larry. He wanted to know exactly how much I would be sending to him and exactly when he would get the check from me. I chose not to engage him. I told him that it would be mailed out to him as soon as I got to it. I didn't have the hours calculated yet so I couldn't tell him off hand what he would be getting back. Larry was getting frustrated with my answers but what the fuck does he expect? He treated me like shit, then tried to blame it on me and when that didn't work I had to get a judge involved to get me the fuck off of his case. He's not high on my list of people that I'm going to drop everything for. Larry wanted a fight and I wasn't having it. I told him that I will be sending him a check and I told him to have a nice day. The part about the check I meant. The part about him having a nice day I didn't.

Over the next few minutes, I received a barrage of texts from Larry. He told me that he wanted to know how much he was getting back. Then he said that I was stealing from him again. He then said that he was headed to my office and we were going to have a discussion. Um, no we weren't, Larry. I decided that I needed to tell him not to text me anymore so that's what I did. I told him to stop texting me and that he wasn't welcome at my office. That was the text that broke Larry's brain. I went to the front door and locked it. I went to the other Nick's office and told him what had happened and to not let a guy who looked like meth head Jesus into the office. Other Nick chuckled when he heard the "meth head Jesus" line. I do have a panache for humor in tense situations. Larry continued to text and then I heard a knock at the front door.

Other Nick said nothing and stood up and calmly walked toward the front door. From inside my office, I heard Larry's voice. I was relieved that other Nick got the door for me. I don't know what I would have done or said to Larry. I felt like a child. I was scared and other Nick was the dad who was going to protect me from the neighborhood bully who looked like meth head Jesus. I'm sorry, but I love the phrase "meth head Jesus." Up until that point, my office had been my sanctuary. It had protected me and given me comfort from the difficult situations and people I had encountered for years. Now this fucking dipshit shows up when I told him he wasn't welcome and ruins it.

Other Nick was great. I didn't poke my head around to see Larry, but I heard other Nick went right at Larry and told him "You and your agents aren't welcome at this office and you need to leave." It was so badass. The former cop in other Nick came out and took control of the situation. Larry didn't say peep and left. From another window, I saw Larry walking around the building and back to his car. I saw that he parked it right behind mine. Larry probably did this so I couldn't leave. I was glad to see him, his mullet, and his girlfriend and driving away.

Unfortunately, other Nick's badassery hadn't stopped the texts from coming. Larry kept firing off text after text. One after another after another. Larry claimed that I was going to steal money from him. He said that I had to tell him how much money he was going to be getting back from me now. "Just give me an estimate," he said. "Can you please give me an estimate so I can plan accordingly?" Even though he did say please this time, fuck Larry and his dumb face. I was going to overbill him, he just knew it.

Then the situation went from crazy to bat shit crazy. Larry texts "Fine, you wanna steal from mental health patients. This isn't over." What the fuck, dude?! We just had court less than an hour ago and you're spewing this bullshit on me over text. You just

148

came to my office when you knew you weren't welcome and then you send me nine texts after I tell you to stop texting me. What else am I supposed to do? After an hour break, he sends me "Please just be fair, Nick." Jesus Christ. I'm so livid. I'm also amused because after calling me a thief, he then flips it up and asks me to be fair.

The guy is a certified mental patient. I absolutely hate his guts. However, I'm not going to steal from anyone. That's not how I roll. I didn't respond to Larry's texts. I thought about calling the police. After Larry left, I felt adrenaline pumping through my hands and forearms. I was on high alert. I was so pissed that I wanted to go find Larry and beat the absolute shit out of him. How dare he come to my office like that? Call me a thief? He was trying to flip all of this onto me. He was the one that was a thief. He was stealing my time and energy. I can only imagine how many times he's done things like this. This wasn't the first time for him, I'm sure of it. Unless he gets his shit together, it's not going to be the last. He's very lucky that I value my license to practice law more than I value some good old fashioned revenge because if I wasn't a lawyer, I would have had no problem confronting Larry when he came to my office and laying hands on that crazy motherfucker. I don't know if I would win or not. I don't really care. Winning would be my goal, however, I would make sure that he thought twice about fucking with me again.

The problem is that times are different than when I grew up. Back in the 90s, guys would resolve their differences and have a physical fight, no weapons involved. As I've gotten older, fights have moved from strictly physical to people fucking around with knives and guns and/or the police being called. That's no fun. I have no idea if Larry had a knife or a gun but he seems like the kind of pussy that would resort to shooting or stabbing someone rather than losing a physical fight.

Larry has me rattled. I am tired of having to deal with this asshole. Now I had to calculate how many hours I had spent on his case and send him money back. That's another thing that has me furious. I should be able to keep the money that he gave me and move on. Now I had to spend more time and write a letter to Larry saying that I'm closing his file with my office. I had to go to the bank to get him a check and I had to spend time figuring out how much time I had spent on his case.

As I was continuing my work for Larry, I stared at my computer and felt depressed. I was adding up the time I had spent and all I wanted was for Larry to go away and leave me the fuck alone. I knew that the sooner I got him his money, the sooner he would be out of my life.

I then realized it wasn't going to matter how much I sent back to him, he was going to be angry no matter what. While I was pissed, I even subtracted some of the time that I had spent on Larry's case because I wanted to make him less pissed. Why did I do that? I shouldn't be afraid of people like Larry. He's a bully that might have some anxiety issues that he's using to manipulate people around him. I should have charged him for every motherfucking second I spent on his case.

I came up with the number of hours and then I wrote a quick letter to Larry letting know that we're done. All the while I am wondering whether he is going to show up at my office again. Larry isn't the kind of person who knows how to think things through. Showing up again when he was told to leave twice seems like a real Larry move.

In the letter, I really wanted to tell Larry what a fucking piece of shit he was, but I didn't. I kept it very matter of fact. The only jab I added to the letter was that based on his unhinged behavior after this morning's hearing, I knew that I made the right decision to withdraw from his case.

I made sure that I documented everything that happened with Larry while things were fresh in my memory. I saved the text messages. I saved all of the emails. I also made sure to add the time that I spent having to interact with him by text over the last week. While earlier I had some reservations about doing that, I decided I should be paid for my time dealing with Larry and his antics. I'm going to get paid for that. I deserve to get paid for that. There are consequences for being an asshole and that's where I was able to hold Larry accountable.

I printed out my closing letter and the detailed statement of my time and threw it in an envelope and went to the bank to get a check for Larry. On the way, I called my wife and told her that maybe it wasn't a good idea for Julian to come to the office today. I had a real nutter on the loose and I don't want Julian being exposed to some crazy asshole like that. Jules understood but I could hear in her voice that she was scared. She wants me to move on from criminal defense so I don't have to deal with people like Larry any longer. I do too.

I got the check, a stamp on the envelope, and put it in the mailbox. I knew that when Larry got this he would reach out again even though I told him to stop texting me. Larry is a little bitch and knows how to try and get under my skin. Well, he did get under my skin but I also knew how to get under his. I wasn't going to respond. What does a crying baby want? Attention. I reached the conclusion that Larry was nothing more than a crying baby. He was going to say or do anything to try and get a reaction from me. What he didn't understand was I am a fantastic lawyer and I also have developed a thicker skin when dealing with people like Larry. I'm not Buddha, I'm not a robot, but I am better than I used to be when I first started being a lawyer. I would have continued to engage Larry by text and email because I wanted to try and win. I realize now that there is no winning in that situation. Larry is going to do what Larry is going to do regardless of what I say or do. My job is to stay in my lane and control how I respond to the situation. While 20 year old me is disappointed that I didn't try and kick Larry's ass when he came over to my office when I told him not to, 20 year old me thought that Limp Bizkit was a great band. So 20 year old me's opinion is flawed on a visceral level. I mean, Nookie is one of the worst songs of all time.

A few days went by and I hadn't heard anything from Larry. It was great. The long Labor Day weekend gave me enough to forget about that miserable piece of shit. He must have gotten the check on Tuesday because Tuesday night he texts me: "Thanks for changing me hundreds of dollars for texting me you piece of shit thief." I was extremely high at the time I got that text and haven't had a laugh like that in months. I was so glad that I was high when he texted me that. I'm sure that Larry sent that text at 7:20pm because he wanted to try and fuck with my evening. Oops, little did he know that I had been hitting my vape pen and was impervious to Larry's bullshit. I guess one of the additional benefits of marijuana, other than helping with my gout, is that it makes me immune to crazy.

The more interactions I had with Larry, the more and more I felt kind of sorry for him. Cue the violins. What went wrong with a person like that? Treating people like shit isn't an overnight thing. It's something that you learn to do over time. I do know one thing, that I slept so well that night. Was it the weed or was I turning a corner with folks like Larry? Probably the weed.

The next day was a busy day of lawyering. Luckily, I didn't have court so I was able to hunker down in the office and get some work done. Then out of the blue, around noon, I got two emails from Larry. Sending multiple texts is bad. Sending multiple emails is the worst. Just send one fucking email, asshole. How fucking pathetic are you?

In his first email, Larry says that he needs me to do something for him. He needs me to send him the videos of the traffic stop that I had received from the prosecutor. The funny thing about that is I already sent them to this asshole. I found it amusing that Larry called me a piece of shit and now he needed something from me. That's cute. Like my entire interaction with Larry, this situation presented me with several options.

First, I could do absolutely nothing. I didn't owe Larry anything. I undercharged him for all the work that I did on his case. I also had to tolerate his wackadoo ass for months. Even Paul Rudd would think this guy is a douchebag. So far, this option was in the lead. The second option was that I could respond back to him and tell him that he could go fuck himself. That one sounded more tempting than doing nothing. However, if I were to do that, that would have shaken even more of the crazy out of Larry and we would end up in a full blown email war, lobbing insults back and forth, spewing hate into the late afternoon and early evening. That option sounded satisfying at first, but then sounded exhausting. It would take a lot of energy to verbally beat the shit out of Larry. Don't get me wrong, It wouldn't be hard because Larry wasn't the kind of person that would woo you with his intellect.

I chose the third option, which was to simply give Larry what he wanted. As usual, I felt like a pussy. All my conditioning and preconceived notions of what I thought it was to be a man required that I fight with this guy so that he knows that he's not going to be taking advantage of me.

STAND UP

I've been in a fog since 2005. I went to law school and I graduated. I graduated in spite of my dad getting esophageal cancer and passing away during my second year. I kept going. I wanted to keep going to make my dad proud of me. In hindsight, he was proud of me no matter what I would have done, except being a mime. In my family, we don't like mimes or magic.

Like any midwestern dad, he didn't give praise all that often. After he died, people would tell me that my dad would tell them how proud he was of me. His son was going to law school in Washington, DC, and he loved that. I wish he didn't have a problem sharing that information with me. Now I understand why. It was because his dad wasn't that way with him either. My grandpa was affectionate with me, but he wasn't with my dad. I think my dad would have absolutely went over the moon for my son had he made it around that long. It's up to me to break that Leydorf cycle of aversion to physical affection to one's spawn.

Continuing to be a lawyer has excruciatingly difficult. Being a criminal defense lawyer and having to go to court and be around people who are low vibe has been the toughest thing that I've had to do. It's not who I really am. I love to create. I love to write, obviously or else I wouldn't have written this book. Being a criminal defense lawyer is nothing like who I am. It's just something that I had to be to get myself out of the mess I created with not thinking things through before I did them.

In my 30s, I became very restless and unhappy with being a lawyer. I was searching for something else. I didn't know who I really was but I knew that something was missing. Going to court and being around the criminal justice system was something that I didn't look forward to doing. Sure, I'd helped a lot of people but I wasn't helping myself.

One day I got a call from someone who said that he wanted to meet with me and talk about guns and how he wanted to make sure he didn't want to get arrested. The message was comically vague. I called the guy back and it ended up being Melik Brown, someone that I am still friends with to this day. He seemed a bit odd on the phone but I was intrigued to meet him. I decided to meet him for coffee and we met at a Bigby in East Lansing.

I was kind of on edge because I didn't know what to expect. Up until that point, my experience with people is that they called me after they committed a crime, not before. It was a bit weird discussing with him what not to do to keep from being arrested. We vibed and became friends.

At the time, he was working on a public access show called Time Slot. He'd been doing that for awhile because after we met, I remembered prank calling the show when I was in college when some friends and I were very, very drunk. It shows you how old I am when I was in college at a time when public access television was a thing. I think my hip just went out and I'm going to go yell at these teenagers to get off my lawn.

Melik and I started hanging out and we'd joke around a lot. I learned that he had done stand up comedy and I thought that was cool. He told me that I should try it. I wanted to, but I was so terrified that I'd be terrible. He was convinced that I wouldn't be. One night, he was going to do a set at an open mic in Ferndale. I don't remember the place. I decided to tag along and he was like "you should put your name on the list when we get there." I was like yeah, sure - having no intention on doing so.

I remember we get to the venue and it was so dark. The people that were on the show were absolutely terrible. I remember being like "see, this is why I'm not doing this thing!" Melik went up and had a good set. You could tell he was working out material but he had that way about him that connected with people.

A couple of months went by and he told me he was starting a show at a place in Old Town Lansing called Sir Pizza. He said it was a contest and that he signed me up and I'd be doing time. I instantly shat my pants in fear. I had no idea what I was going to say. My wife was going to kill me because she had just given birth to Julian a few months before and here I am leaving her to do open mic comedy.

I had a couple of weeks to prepare and I got more and more nervous by the day. It's so weird, I got so much more nervous for stand up than I ever had going to court. For lawyering, I guess if I fucked up at least I wouldn't be going to jail. With stand up, if I fucked up I was convinced I was going to die.

I started writing some things down in a notebook to get ready. They were basically observations about being a dad. Things that I had experienced like when Julian was born. I had no idea what I was doing. I'd never done anything like this before. I wasn't in plays or anything like that in school. I had made people laugh before but that was just me acting like a jackass or intentionally falling down. I had no idea how I was going to translate that into 7 minutes of me standing up in front of a group of strangers.

Unfortunately, when I ran it by Jules she told me that I should go for it. I was really hoping that she was going to put the kibosh on the whole thing and then I'd have a way out. I'd tell Melik that my shrew of a wife won't let me do stand up and I'd be able to get out of it. But no, she had to be all supportive and everything. The nerve of that woman!

The only way out of it was to either fake my death or to actually cancel. I didn't want to let Melik down. I think deep down that this was something that I had wanted to do for awhile. I had never really been into stand up itself as an art form. I remember my parents watching Bill Cosby's stand up and laughing. That didn't age well... But I'm not like other people who'd been exposed to Richard Pryor or George Carlin. I loved funny things like watching Robin Williams act like a fool or watching Chris Farley fall down and break things. I was looking for an out to the mundanity of being a lawyer and Melik put one in front of me.

The day of the show came and I was an absolute wreck. I had worked myself up into absolute panic. I went back and forth between mania and paralysis. Oh, and the stress had given me diarrhea too, which was lovely. I spent half the day on the toilet. At least it gave me some peace and quiet from a screaming infant. Julian is great now at 13 years old, but holy shit he was a real jerk when he was a baby.

Jules saw me during the day and was like "Jesus Christ, it's just a show, calm down!" This from a classically trained opera singer who just pooped a baby out of her vagina a few months prior. She's performed in Italy and has gone through the most difficult thing a person can do and survived. She wasn't relatable to me. I also drank a lot of coffee that day which meant more nerves and diarrhea.

She drove me to the show because I was too nervous. I was absolutely freaking out. I kept pacing around and people were trying to talk with me but all I would say was "oh, that's nice." My mom and step dad stayed at home to watch Julian.

Everything was a blur before the show. I have seen pictures and I saw what I was wearing and I'm embarrassed for me. I was wearing a baby blue shirt that said "Say Yes to Michigan" on it and I was wearing shorts. I broke the cardinal rule of standup which is don't wear shorts on stage. I had no idea of my crime at the time but now I would have rolled my eyes at myself. I was also wearing orange shoes which were distracting. More distracting were my handsome gams. It's unfortunate that the first rule of stand up is don't wear shorts on stage because I have fantastic legs. They're shapely and not too hairy.

I went up and did my time and I have to say it wasn't half bad. I know, you must be thinking that this is a guy with a real fragile ego and he's going to tell us it was good even if he went up there and tried to fuck the mic stand. On my honor, which according to Larry I'm a piece of shit thief, I tell you that it wasn't bad. Other than the unforgivable error of wearing shorts it wasn't the worst thing that's ever happened to stand up comedy.

Comedians will tell you that it can go one of two ways when you first do stand up. You either do amazing, or you eat a steaming plate of shit for 5 minutes. I have seen both with my own two eyes. I can tell you that I didn't do shittily.

After that first time doing it, I was hooked. I'd never had that same experience before. It was such an adrenaline rush. The same kind that happened when I was dealing with shitheads like Larry and the guy who wanted to kill me but it was a different feeling. I really felt alive. It's the closest thing to being chased by a sabretooth tiger that we're going to experience in the modern world.

After the show I was looking around like "ok so does an agent just get ahold of me, or what?" I had advanced to the finals of the competition. I didn't come in first but moving on was enough of a positive experience that I wanted to do more.

I didn't sleep much that night. I was tossing and turning and oh yeah we had a baby in the house that wouldn't sleep at all. The pure joy from doing that show wasn't the kind of feeling that I experienced when my son was born or when I got married to Jules but it came in a close third.

I talked about what I knew. I didn't have well written jokes. There was no "take my wife, please" kind of stuff. It was basically me having held in years of thoughts that I didn't share with anyone and me standing up there in my shorts and baby blue shirt nervously pacing around the stage.

Being a frustrated dad was the thing that I tapped into the first time that I went on stage. I was able to write down a few thoughts and I actually came up with a few good jokes. One was how I was going to share a secret with parents of newborns about how I got my son to sleep through the night. That usually gets the people paying attention who were like me and had a kid that was up all night like he was doing lines of coke and drinking Code Red Mountain Dew. I said I found out a secret to get my son to sleep through the night. I've found that he'll never wake me up when I go to sleep with headphones on. It's silly and cute but hey that's me, dammit!

I wish I could go back and bottle the joy that I experienced after the first time I did stand up. I was pacing around still and was encouraging everyone else that was on the show and inside I had felt that attention that I hadn't gotten growing up. It felt amazing to be able to do something as simple as talk into a microphone and the end result was a group of people laughing and with that came a feeling of acceptance. Sure, I had no idea what I was doing but it was that feeling you have when you're with someone new and it's all amazing. I thought I had found what I wanted to do that night in Sir Pizza in Old Town Lansing.

After the show they announced that the finals were going to be the next month at the same place. That means I had a month to get my set ready. Having done stand-up that one time, I was terrified again. Can't we just cut to the scene where they award me the trophy? I think that would be much easier. But you can't do that in life and oh yeah there wasn't a trophy we were getting a free pizza or something like that.

One good thing that I did was record that set. I can't find it anymore but I listened to what I did over and over to pick out the pieces that worked so I could do them again. I thought, why reinvent the wheel. Just wear some pants this time, get up there and do what worked and get your pizza and get the fuck outta there.

However, my ego made what would be its first of many appearances in my stand-up career. I was doubting myself. You shouldn't do the same material over again, you need to come back with something fresh and new! Little did I know that most stand up comedians when they first start find the jokes that work and do them over and over again. I put time into writing things down that I thought would be funny but I didn't plan things out about how I would test them out. I found out very quickly that my wife had an extremely low tolerance for me testing new jokes on her when we had a screaming crying baby in the house that hated sleep.

What could be better for my anxiety than not preparing for your second ever stand up set, right? The day came and I again was paralyzed with fear. Even more than the first time that I went up. I texted Melik and told him that I wasn't feeling well. He told me to get my ass to the show. I was nervous but then I weighed my options - stay at home with a crying baby or go bomb in front of a group of strangers. I shit out what I thought was the last of my pre-show diarrhea and headed to Sir Pizza.

The nerves gave me tunnel vision. Melik was trying to talk with me but I was giving him the 1,000 yard stare and shifting my weight back and forth from one leg to the other. I don't think I sat down the entire time. I was just pacing in the back.

I saw some new people that I hadn't seen from the first show. I panicked and was like "these are new people just do the stuff from the first show that worked!" That meant I was switching things up minutes before I was going to go on, which didn't do any wonders for my anxiety.

Melik went up and called my name. People clapped and I walked up and I don't remember what I said for the next 5 to 7 minutes. I do remember that the fear and anxiety melted away as soon as I took the mic out of the mic stand. I did my time, people clapped. I didn't feel as good about how I did the first time but I had to wait and see how everyone else did. I didn't see any professional comedians doing a show in Lansing on a Sunday night for a free pizza so I thought I had a shot at winning.

Well, I didn't win. It turned out that a local TV anchor had moved on in the other round before mine. He promoted the show on TV and had 70% of the audience there just for him. I didn't know that at the time. All I knew is that I saw some dude go up and take the mic and then do a lip synced version of some Men At Work song and a bunch of middle aged women went nuts.

I was like "what the fuck?!" That's not comedy, that's just some dude shucking and jiving his way around the stage dancing to some 80s song. I could have done that. It wasn't the first time that I felt I didn't get what I deserved in comedy, and it wouldn't be the last. My ego has a way of doing that.

Standup is a high risk, high reward endeavor. There's so many things that can happen to make it go wrong. I've done shows in bars where people are playing pool during the show. Yeah, that's not going to work. At that same show, I had a biker gang come into the bar during my set and started playing pool with their 8 year old son who was wearing biker leathers. God damn, it's like 10:30 at night. That kid should be at home in bed and not going through lesson one of the Sons of Anarchy guide to being a shithead.

Standup isn't like bowling. It's not something that you can just show up and do once a month with your friends. You have to consistently work on writing and editing and getting to the bottom of your feelings. Some people just want to show up and go up and by some divine intervention they are going to get shot with a laser beam of funny and they'll spew out hilarious material and the crowd will carry them off the stage. That's not going to happen.

It's funny but the more I got into stand up the more complicated I discovered it to be. Maybe I'm wrong, but there's so much going on. There's so much that you have to be paying attention to when you're up there. It's like having 8 Google Chrome tabs open in your brain and each one of them is doing their own thing. You have to be keeping track of your time. You have to be reading the room to see whether people are enjoying what you're doing. You have to know where you're at in the show, are they going to drop off the check for the audience? If so, then you have to do something to keep their attention. What's the body language going on with the dude up here in the front. Why are his arms crossed? What's his deal. It can be fun and exhausting at the same time. I know that I did a great job when at the end I'm sweating from the top of my head and I feel a bit like I just played 8 hours of video games straight.

I've now been doing stand up for 8 years and it's one of those things where I never know where I am with it. I love doing it more than anything that I've ever done. It is also a lot of work. I have to put myself out there on a consistent basis and opening myself up to potential failure. That's not something that I did regularly in my life before stand up. I never really had a doubt about becoming a lawyer. I didn't know what I wanted to do with it but I never thought that I wouldn't be able to succeed at it. With stand up, I know what I want to do which is be able to do shows in front of thousands of people and put out albums that people enjoy and the material that I discuss resonates with them.

Like anything, stand up is something that you have to keep showing up. There have been times that I didn't want to do shows but I did them anyway because I saw it as all part of a goal. My "career" has been a bunch of tiny Lego bricks that over time I made into a tiny wall. I never did anything that was amazing. It was a series of small victories and also eating some shit sandwiches.

Stand up is a distraction from the other life that I built for myself that I haven't enjoyed it. Because stand up is something that you need to do a lot in order to be good, it means that you either have to spend a lot of time working at it or you're going to be mediocre at it. If you do it half assed, then you're never going to get any good at it. I was doing it at least 2-3 times per week at night and then going getting up and going to work at 8am. I don't know anyone who was fucking doing that. A lot of my stand up contemporaries are young and don't have full time careers or families. Oh yeah, I almost forgot. On top of doing stand up and being a full time lawyer, I was also a husband and a father. It's been hard at times to be able to balance my two jobs and a family. It's like one of those things where it's caused some strife in my marriage. I get it. Stand up is one of those things that you see people do but you don't know how much work it takes. My wife wasn't exactly thrilled when I told her that I wanted to start doing this when we had a newborn in the house.

However, I needed stand up in order to maintain my sanity. In addition to it probably being something that I needed to do in order to feel whole, it's a distraction that I needed to get over the bullshit that I've experienced being a lawyer. Having to trudge through the fucking idiots who want to steal your time and energy is tough, so let's get a distraction that makes you pay all of the attention to it or you're going to absolutely suck at it.

My wife wasn't always supportive of me pursuing comedy. When I was fitting in 3 sometimes 4 shows per week she was letting me know that it wasn't cool with her. She was making it exceedingly difficult for me to live at the house she'd give me a bunch of shit about it. Looking back, I was pretty obsessed. I wanted this very badly. I felt like I had to make up for the late start that I got. Some people that I work with in comedy had been doing it since they were 18 years old. If I had 18 years at stand up and I wasn't able to do exactly what I wanted to with it, I would have probably quit because it meant that I'm fucking terrible at it. My wife got pissed one time and also had a moment of understanding. She meshed the two into a conversation that we had. She said "Listen, if you're going to spend a bunch of time away from home doing then, they you better get fucking good at it." That's the way Jules is. She comes from a performance background so she'll watch something that someone would say "that's good" and she'll watch the same thing and say "umm is that the best you could make it?" I actually life that. While it does mean I take a few hits from the ego every fiscal year, it does also mean that I am always striving to get better. Like that movie "Whiplash," there's no two worse words in the English language than "good job."

People have given me shit about doing comedy and it makes me real easy to distance myself from them. It's one of those things that consumes you. I had a friend who's sister became obsessed with running and joined a cult. Stand up for me is kind of like that. It's something that other people don't understand but the people that are in stand up completely understand how awesome it is and why you'd want to devote your life to it. When some people talk to me that aren't in stand up they use the word "hobby," and I fucking hate that. Listen, Jim, it's not bowling, it's stand up. I'm not doing this for shits and giggles and as some part of a midlife crisis. There are easier ways to have a mid-life crisis that don't involve you getting up in front of a bunch of strangers and try to make them laugh.

Don't get me wrong, there have been some times where I've absolutely hated stand up. One night in 2014, I did a show in Belding, Michigan at this place called the Candlestone Resort. It was a golf course and a hotel in this little town called Belding, Michigan. I never understood why they had a hotel and a golf course in the middle of fucking nowhere, but I didn't care because they put on regular comedy shows there.

I had messaged the booker and wanted to do a set on a Friday night, so I could show him what I could do, so he'd book me at that room to do a longer set. He said that was cool, so I drove the hour there. I got free food and was going to get paid like $25. Nothing major. At that point, it was cool to get paid to do stand-up at all. I get to the venue a bit early and meet the booker, and we talk for a bit. I ask him what the crowd is like and go over how much time I'm going to be doing. The headliner was an older guy from Chicago, whom I had never met before. He got there right before showtime, and we were sitting at the same table. Venues generally have a specified table for the comedians. They like to keep us separate, like the kids' table at Thanksgiving. They don't want us to mingle with the paying guests, I guess.

This headliner was a fucking douchebag. He was throwing around names of people that he'd performed with and trying to rub it in my face. I told him that I had started a couple of years ago. He jumps in with a story about how he performed with some old dude I hadn't heard of when he was two years in. He was an older middle-aged white guy, you know, the kind of guy that caused all of the problems that people are fighting to overcome now. One of those people that liked to brag about themselves. They ask a general question and you can tell from the look of their dumb face that they're not listening to what you're saying, they're just waiting for them to interject something about themselves.

The show started, and it was a crowd full of dumb older white people. There's nothing wrong if you're that kind of person. Okay, sorry I lied. If you're old and you only get your news from FOX News, then there is something wrong with you. This was the kind of crowd where someone could yell the n-word, and there's a good chance no one would think it was that big of a deal.

I'm up there and I'm doing my thing. It's honestly not going great. I understand that using multisyllabic words and having punchlines that aren't just saying "women be shopping" or "you gotta beat your kids" just isn't for everyone. I'm not doing amazing. I'm not really bombing either. Unfortunately, I made the mistake of not looking at my watch when I went up on stage. Usually, the person running the show will give you a light when it's time for you to wrap up. The booker didn't give me the light so I just kept going. I went through all of the material that I had at that point without really knowing it. I thought maybe he needed me to go longer, like maybe because the old white headliner douche had a stroke or shit his pants and I needed to go longer. The show runner got my attention off to the side of the room and I ended really quickly. As I'm walking to the back of the room, I see the headliner walk up and he says "pay attention you might learn something." It wasn't one of those things that comedians say to fuck around with someone. This guy wasn't joking. This guy told me that there's a myth that comedians aren't successful with money because he drives an Audi. Jesus Christ, dude. How insecure is this guy? He's in his late 50s and according to him he's been doing stand up since the dawn of time and has opened for Jesus. Yet, he felt the need to put me down. I felt really small after that. I guess I had done pretty bad, but it happens. I really just wanted to leave but I had to stick around to get paid.

I sat and watched this guy, and he was terrible. However, he was getting laughs. The dumb white people were eating this shit up, in addition to the salad bar.

While I hate to admit it, comedy isn't just fun – it is emotional survival. It provides a lifeline to allow me to say what I want and felt like I couldn't say in court or at home. The pursuit of laughter is nothing more than attempt to fill that deep hole within – the hug I didn't get as a kid.

Opening Statements

I remember being in the bathroom for so long that the automatic lights went out. The time spent in the bathroom was probably a product of my not wanting to start this trial and the Indian food that my wife had made the night before. As your lawyer, I'd strongly recommend that you don't eat Indian food the night before a murder trial, unless you're Indian. There's no more helpless feeling than being in the bathroom when the automatic lights go out. I stepped outside of the stall with my pants around my ankles, waving my hand like a madman trying to get this motion light to turn back on. The idiot who decided to put a timed light in the bathroom has never pooped before. Luckily, none of the jurors happened to come into the bathroom at that moment. If they did, we'd definitely have to start the trial over and pick a new jury. If one of the jurors tells the judge "Your Honor, I saw Mr. Leydorf in the bathroom with his pants around his ankles waving at me." Is this true counsel? Yes, your honor. Okay then, that's a wrap.

After I gather what's left of my dignity, I wash my hands and take a look at myself in the mirror. The gravity of what is happening catches up to me all at once, like when you touch an exposed wire. Is this my life? I never wanted to be a litigator. I never wanted to set foot in a courtroom, for that matter. I wanted to be a boring corporate lawyer who reviewed contracts and had a cushy life. Here I am staring at myself in a mirror in St. Johns, Michigan, ready to start a murder trial by myself. I never felt so alone.

There's no time for feeling sorry for myself, though. Next up is the opening statements. I had worked on what I was going to say to the jury more than I had ever worked on an opening statement. It's hard to write a persuasive statement in a vacuum like that. In the weeks before trial, I was in my office imagining the jury box full of attentive people hanging on my every word. In my daydream, there was a black lady in the back row of the jury box fanning herself. She was tagging every one of my sentences with an "Amen!" or "Go ahead now!" like it was church. After I finished and thanked the jury for their time, every one of them stood and said in unison, "Not Guilty!" Then my client gives me a high five and we all go out for beers.

Unfortunately, what I had imagined and what actually happened were vastly different. In a criminal trial, the prosecutor gets to deliver their opening statement first. Whenever I listen to a prosecutor talk, I really have to control my facial expressions. I turn into Anderson Cooper trying to get through a Trump press conference. I think it's my eyebrows. Because I'm bald, those fuckers are more noticeable. Then I'll add a deep sigh like a toddler being told they have to go to their room.

Before I knew it, it was my turn. I did what I always do when I have prepared notes - I didn't fucking pay attention to them at all. I just went off. Hindsight being 20/20, it's not the best strategy when you're dealing with a case as serious as this. It wasn't a great time to be shooting from the hip. I realize that's a poor choice of words, but whatever. That's what I did. I was riled up by the prosecutor's opening statement. Their statement didn't have to be 15 minutes long. All he had to do was stand up and say "the evidence is going to show you that this guy fucking did it" and sit down. If he had done that, I wouldn't have gotten as pissed as I did. However, he played around with the facts, twisting them more than your drunk uncle does when recounting his high school football glory days. He pissed me off. It was like the beginning of any kind of sporting event where one team knew that the other was better than them. This guy wasn't better than me, but he had all the facts. He had all the players that he needed to crush my case, but he decided to get flashy. He tried to run a double reverse pass on the first play. The anger woke me up, like the first time you get hit in the face. The first time I was punched in the face was in 6th grade by James Chapko. He hit me right in the nose. It instantly made my eyes water. It's not a good look, but I was ready to rumble after I wiped the tears away and insisted, "I'm not crying!". Now you're ready. The goal of being in a silk stocking corporate law firm was over. I was in the trenches, and I wanted to win more than ever.

I came out of my blackout about 10 minutes later and thanked the jury for their time. I gathered my notes and started to walk back to my chair. I stopped and went back to the podium and told them, "I want to ask only one thing of you. I want you to pay attention." Then I walked back to my seat. As I sat down, I could feel the energy in the room shift. There were some court staff in the room that hadn't seen me in action in court before, and I could tell that I just changed their opinions of me, in a good way. My ass sweat rapidly decreased after standing for 10 minutes and was now out of critical levels, down to 48%.

After my opening statement, it was the prosecutor's show. They had to start building a case against my client, who I still couldn't believe wanted to go to trial. There was enough evidence to convince ten juries' worth of people that he did this beyond a reasonable doubt. Nevertheless, I had to move past that. That was his decision to make, not mine. I can't force people to make smart decisions. I can't make people help themselves. Even years after this trial is over, I still think about the decision he made, and I'm not sure why he made it. I find myself in this job trying to save people. Sometimes people don't want to be saved.

The prosecutor starts off by calling the guys who say that they were with my client when the robbery and murder happened. That's probably a good place for them to start. Honestly, it's hard to imagine a bad place for them to start, given all of the evidence that they had. It's hard to put that into words, and I know I'm belaboring the point, but there was a shitload of evidence. Yes, that's a legal term of art.

While the prosecutor is asking his snitches questions, I have pages and pages of notes on important points to make. I have references to lines in transcripts of their prior testimony and photos. All ready to destroy them. I sat patiently in my chair and waited. This was probably the only time in my life that I felt like Mr. Miyagi. As the trial went on, my anxiety lessened. My ass sweat percentage continued to decrease as I became more locked into the moment and was present with what was unfolding around me. This huge spectacle is happening not more than ten feet away, and I'm sitting there trying to catch a fly with these chopsticks.

Make no mistake, I'm not the kind of person who is braggadocios. Hell, I don't even like that word. It sounds pretentious. I'm the "just the facts, ma'am" kind of guy. No filler, just give me the information. My wife pulls her hair out because I often answer questions with just a "yes" or "no." She often gets pissed off at me and has said many times, "God dammit, give me some fucking details!" That's not how I roll, fam. So I'm not here to say that I'm fucking Buddha or anything like that. It was strange how the anxiety melted away when I sat and took each moment on as it came. My anxiety lessened the less I thought about what was going to happen next.

There was a theme underlying the testimony of each one of these dudes. In addition to not having a strong command of the English language, they all had one thing in common. Each one of them was getting a deal in exchange for their testimony. This kind of thing happens often in criminal cases. Two friends will work together and rob a little old lady, or they're entrepreneurs and they decide to start a small, locally sourced, meth making business. One idiot gets arrested. That idiot gets questioned by the police and spills the beans. That idiot will agree to testify against the other idiot. In exchange, Idiot #1 will get a lesser sentence. Idiot #2 gets fucked. The deal that they all got was how I was going to discredit them.

There were many other things that I could have used to make the cross-examination last for days, but I decided to focus on that one point. I've also learned from being a stand-up comedian for 9 years that it's hard to hold people's attention. Sure, people at the Chuckle Hut are typically drunk, but still, people these days have the attention span of a gnat on coke. My thinking was I was going to be hard to keep the jury's attention if I tried to make 1,000 points over 18 hours of cross-examination. No one wants to slog through that (cue the "Ain't nobody got time for that" meme). Honestly, when I watch other attorneys in court cross-examine a witness, I get bored because they're trying to do too much. Mark Twain said, "Brevity is the soul of wit." It applies in comedy just the same as in cross-examination. Attorneys feel they have to do it all and cover each and every point, but it gets so goddamn boring to listen to. Know your audience is another comedy axiom that applies to law, too. A lot of people can't fucking stand lawyers to begin with. After you try and ask the same question 23 times, people are going to tune out.

If I kept it simple, I thought that I could make them think that every time I asked one of these guys a question, it was going to be how they were getting a deal for testifying. Many of them changed their stories from the original ones that they told to the detectives. I had to paint them as lying pieces of shit. With all the lies they told, they basically gave me the brushes and the paint; I just had to Rembrandt this motherfucker for the jury.

Having chosen where I wanted to go, I needed to work backwards from there. What was nice was that I had good evidence to show that they were all communicating with each other after they were arrested. A couple of these sacks of shit were being held in the same jail. It's not too much of a stretch to assume that they were talking to each other. It's probably also not a stretch to assume that they were talking about this murder that just happened, and not the latest season of Grey's Anatomy. One of the best facts was that one of the co-defendants' girlfriends (I hate saying "baby mama") had a relationship with my client. BINGO! The guy who was in jail wanted to get my client in jail so he wouldn't make sweet, sweet love with his girlfriend. What better way to get a jury's attention than a plot for a smutty romance novel?

As the witnesses seemed to fly by, I was feeling increasingly confident. It was because there was no pressure on me to win this. This was the prosecutor's case to lose. I was sticking with my strategy. Make these piles of garbage out to be piles of garbage to the jury. What I should have anticipated, but didn't, was that each one of the snitches wanted to argue with me during cross-examination. I guess there's something about being a snitch in a murder case that turns one into a self-righteous witness. Rather than get angry, I simply poured on the country charm that I buried years ago because I thought being folksy wasn't intellectual. Turns out you can't take the boy out of the mobile home. By deflecting their snide comments, I made them look like the ones who wanted a fight, not me. If they didn't have anything to hide, why were they trying to start a fight with me? I wanted to convey to the jury that I just wanted to get to the bottom of this. Honestly, I wasn't shoveling bullshit either. I honestly did want to know what happened here. The months of prep made me doubt the narrative that the prosecutor was laying out for the jury. It was like I was the VC and they were the Americans in Vietnam. I had to fight a guerrilla war. I didn't have much ammo to work with. I had to make each bullet count. It was easy for me to take shots at them because their big old pieces of evidence lumbered along and weren't very maneuverable.

The trial was flying by, and the judge said we could take a break for lunch. I had been working hard, so I decided to treat myself. Of course, I went to Subway. I got a footlong. I'm not trying to brag, but I was going to be getting paid 60 bucks an hour defending this guys life, so hell yeah I was going to get a footlong club on wheat, toasted, provolone cheese, spinach (not lettuce because I'm a fancy boy) tomato, pickle and yellow pepper with one line of southwest sauce. Oh, and also chips and a drink. As I reflect on my go-to Subway order, I realize how I got gout in the first place.

Instead of sitting alone inside, I decided to sit alone in my car and listen to music. I didn't want to mingle with the jurors because, as I was checking out, I saw a few of them starting to come inside the building to get their cold, soulless, and depressing Subway sandwich. No one is ever happy in a Subway. It smells of regret, and that tuna that we all know isn't really tuna.

Because of the stupid old lady in front of me, I had less than an hour before things started up again. This old lady in front of me ordered two subs (of course, with a coupon, why would you even ask that?) and did the thing that some people do when they're next in line - completely forget where the fuck they are or what they're doing. She's up next, and when the Sandwich Artist with the neck tattoo asked her, "What can I get started for you today?" she responded with a blank stare. "Umm, I'd like spaghetti. Do you have spaghetti?" What the fuck?! Ma'am, I'm gonna shove your old ass out of the way unless you get your shit together real quick. You've had 89 years to work out what you get when you go to Subway.

With a belly full of Subway sandwich, I didn't feel nervous. Turns out a footlong sub is like Zoloft for me. Ass sweat concentration was at an optimal level - less than 5%. The fact that my ass was drenched earlier was almost a distant memory.

I got back to the courthouse and walked back inside the electronic doors with a pep in my step that hadn't been there in years. A deputy asked me, "How are things going up there?" "I don't know, I was asleep all morning!" I said. It made him chuckle. I like making the old deputies laugh. They're usually retired police officers, so they've seen some shit. If you make them laugh, it's typically a solid joke.

I was feeling alive as a lawyer for the first time in a long time. Maybe being a lawyer was my purpose in life? Maybe I was meant to suffer through this in order to fulfill my destiny? Ugh, destiny sounds pretentious, but you get it. Maybe this is what my life is supposed to be like. Perhaps the ass sweat, the living in my head, and self-doubt were just parts of me, and the quicker I learned to live with them, the easier this bus stop of a life would be?

I settled in for an afternoon of guerrilla lawyering. The best way to describe the next witness was that he was "the white guy" of the group. I found him particularly annoying. This was the first time that I had the pleasure of meeting him. I had only read the transcript of his testimony at the preliminary examination. He was trying to come off like he was a badass. Simply reading what he had to say produced an audible "UGH!" when I was reading them in my office.

The prosecutor announced that the white guy would be the next witness. The deputy brought him out from the holding cell through a side door in the courtroom. It took a while for the white guy to get to the witness stand because he was pimp limping his way across the courtroom. The deputy asked him, "Do you swear to tell the truth, the whole truth, and nothing but the truth, so help me God?" The white guy said yes. I had to keep my eyes from completely rolling into the back of my head because this guy had been questioned several times and testified under oath at a previous hearing, and no two stories were the same. Not only was he an unlikable person, but he was also a liar.

The prosecutor opened the questioning with some pleasantries. Not sure why because this dude was a straight-up thug, or at least he fancied himself as one. You would have had better luck trying to polish a turd than to pass this guy off as a productive member of society. "How are you doing?" Come on, man! The guy is a snitch in a murder trial. He's had better days.

There were many reasons why I didn't like the white guy. If I had to pinpoint one, I didn't like him because he was trying to be something that he wasn't. He created a facade. This wasn't who he was. In addition to perjury, he was also guilty of cultural appropriation. I was trying to be something I'm not, too, a lawyer, but at least I didn't tag everything I said with "you know what I'm sayin'?"

I think it was Bill Burr that said that if there's one white guy in a group of black guys, the white guy is the crazy motherfucker. He had to prove that he belonged in the group and probably had to do some fucked up shit to earn respect. This was definitely true with this white guy. He bragged about his familiarity with guns. He even bragged that he was an expert in firearms. I read that with a chuckle and appreciated the tongue-in-cheek in which it must have been delivered in public. The irony of this guy, who was so hard but was a snitch, wasn't lost on me either.

As the direct examination continued, the prosecutor was lobbing softball after softball. My contempt for the white guy continued to build. I fantasized about him having to excuse himself because he got diarrhea from drinking the toilet wine he made back at the jail. "Your Honor, I pooped my pants!" Then everyone stood up and laughed, and pointed at him as the young people filmed it on their phones. Then, out of nowhere, the prosecutor asked the question that would fuck up the entire trial. It unraveled the months of work that I'd put in preparing for this case. The prosecutor started down a line of questioning about how this idiot knew my client. The prosecutor asked, "Had you heard that (my client) had killed other people?" Dude. What. The. Fuck? Time slowed down. My heart started racing, and my vision narrowed. The witness said, "Yup, I heard he killed people before." Something inside my brain asked, "Wait, what the fuck did this guy just ask the witness?"

Relationships

The stress of being a lawyer has wreaked havoc on my capacity to begin and sustain personal relationships. In law school, it meant that I didn't have many friends. I had no interest in hanging out with anyone associated with law school because I associated law school with death, and no one wants to hang out with the Grim Reaper, sorry, Dale, or whatever the Grim Reaper's actual name is.

Also, being in Miami, I was 1,400 miles away from all of my high school and college friends back in Michigan. I didn't make time for those relationships because I was trying to figure out law school and keep my head above water. As a result, those relationships suffered. I felt alienated. I was going through a huge odyssey with a group of people who were in my law school class, but I didn't want anything to do with them outside of law school. I wanted to have my own life outside of law school that didn't involve those people. Aside from Mike Elliot, I didn't associate with anyone down in Miami. I would go to school, I would come home, and I would hang out with Jules. That was it.

In the few times that I carved out for myself, Mike and I would go work out at the fitness center at the University of Miami. It was the most luxurious gym that I've ever seen. Everyone there was so good-looking. Where were all of these hot people hiding? They weren't in law school, that's for sure. It made the people who passed for aesthetically pleasing back in Michigan look like 3s and 4s. It seemed like everyone on campus at the U was like an 8. I guess the oppressive heat and being 6 inches from the sun will mold you into someone you'd see in an Aqua Di Gio perfume ad.

It turns out, Mike was an amazing squash player. He played squash for the Naval Academy. I didn't know the U.S. Naval Academy had a squash team. I thought they'd be busy playing Battleship or whatever they do on submarines. He wanted me to come try it with him one day. I had never played squash before. Aside from one year of tennis my freshman year of high school, I didn't have much experience with racket sports. It showed. Even though I was in pretty decent shape, I felt like I was going to die there on that squash court, keel over in front of all these hot people.

While I was looking for a way to get out my frustration of dealing with the immersion into the foreign land that is law school, all that I got was a frustrating afternoon of chasing a stupid ball around the court. Mike absolutely destroyed me. He was amazing at squash, tennis, oh and also ping pong. We had a rec area at school where you could play ping pong, and he destroyed me at that every time we played. In a word, I was frustrated.

Things were difficult at home, too. Jules had taken a year off from school after getting into every music conservatory that she wanted. That was difficult to deal with for me. I busted my ass to get into all of these law schools, and she gets into these amazing schools, and it didn't seem like she even had to try. When she did get into the top schools, she decided to take a year off.

Before she came down to Miami, I had several conversations with her about what I was going to need if she was going to come down there. I was going to have to be hyper-focused on school, and I wasn't going to have much time for a relationship. It wasn't personal. I loved her so much. It was just that I needed as much time as possible to figure law school out, and I was going to need every waking minute to do that. She said she was cool with that, but I knew that there would be times when it would be difficult for her.

We are both only children. For me, that meant that I had a lot of space growing up. I was left on my own to do my own thing. It was very lonely. My mom and dad would leave me in my room, and we each would be doing our own things. I don't want to make it out like they weren't around. They were. We would have dinner together every night in the kitchen. But we wouldn't do a lot of talking about our feelings and emotions. I guess it was the typical midwestern thing where we would remain on the surface with things and not bring up our own emotions.

Not having a sibling in that environment stunted my emotional growth. I didn't talk about my emotions much with my parents, and my typical reaction when something bad happened would be to have a meltdown. One night, I remember punching a hole in my door. I didn't get in trouble for it either. No one even really mentioned it. It was kind of glossed over, and then later they joked with me about it.

Jules had an opposite-only-child experience from what I had. Her parents had been together for many, many years, but were no longer living together. They were still married, but they lived in separate houses. They had split up and gotten back together many times. When I met them when Jules and I had first started dating back in college, they were still living together, but shortly after that, they split up, and I don't think they ever lived together again.

Jules's mom was an American citizen who was born in India. Her mom's parents were missionaries in India, and they raised 5 children in India. Jules's dad was Indian. He is a professional violinist and a huge asshole.

It's sad because he wasn't always an asshole. When I first met him, he seemed like a pretty good guy. We would talk about basketball; he loves the NBA, and I felt like we got along pretty well. As I kept dating Jules, I came to find out that Jules's parents didn't have such a great relationship and that Jules's dad was the cause for much of that.

I had never met an Indian person before. They didn't have Indian people in Bannister. All they have in Bannister is the generic white version of a person. If people were bread, people in Bannister were that white bread that you get at the fish fry place, and Indians are chapati, you get it. The first time I went to their house, I remember taking off my shoes. That was something that we didn't really do in my house. If we had shoes on in the house, it wasn't a big deal. Now that I think of it, it's pretty fucking gross to wear shoes in the house. You're walking around all day stepping in disgusting shit, and then you bring it into your house and just walk around? Gross. I don't know why we did that in our family, and it's not like we talked about that either.

The thing that really impressed me was that Jules's dad was an amazing cook. The first time that I met them, they invited me over for an amazing Indian meal. I had no idea what to expect, because again, we didn't have Indian food in Bannister. It was the generic meat and potatoes kind of bullshit. The kind of cooking where if someone did use spices, you'd ask what they put in something to make it taste so good, and they'd be like, "salt."

Jules's dad and mom did the cooking, but over the years, Jules's dad would really make some amazing Indian food for me. Chicken Dopiaza, Saag Paneer (he would make his own mother fucking cheese), Onion Pakora, Naan. You name it, and he could cook it.

The first time I had Indian food, it blew my mind. Hours later, it would also blow out my colon. I had never shit like that before in my life. Dollars to donuts, I am positive no Indian has ever experienced the sensation of constipation. All of that spicy rumbling around in your belly means that you're never going to be blocked up. Maybe it was just my overactive gut, but whenever I have Indian food, I shit my brains out.

As the relationship with Jules progressed, I learned that her mother and father were exceedingly difficult people. They argued a lot and fought a lot. I wouldn't see it when I was there, but for Jules, it was a regular occurrence to see her parents fight. I lucked out in that regard. I never saw Jeff and Kathy fight. Looking back, I would have loved to see some fucking emotion; it would have broken up the monotony of being an only child in a house where people didn't directly talk about their feelings. In my household, there was, however, an abundance of that good ol' midwestern passive aggressiveness. A lot of, "Oh, that's nice," when shit wasn't nice.

As a result of their challenging family dynamics, Jules developed a tight-knit relationship with her mother. Even more than the typical bond that a mother has with their daughter. Her mom would often get on my nerves because she was so different from anyone that I had ever been around before. Instead of liking peace and quiet, she would talk. Like a lot. Like more than any person that I've ever been around before. It would get to the point where I'd be like "damn, woman, don't you ever stop talking?" I had never experienced anything like that. And she was so animated. She was very in your face and wanted to know exactly what you were thinking. It made me really tired and anxious to be around her.

Jules and I are quite different in that way. I like to be by myself, and she likes to be with people. I don't know how we have made it work, but we have. Miami was difficult for both of us, though. I don't know why I decided to go to law school down in Miami, but I am glad I did because it has led me to the path that I'm currently on. Had I not gone down to Miami, who knows what I would be doing now? I would have probably just gone to MSU for law school and not had the experience of living on my own. Truth be told, I would probably not have had so much in student loan debt, and that's the only thing that I really regret.

Jules and I started arguing a lot in Miami. I was under a tremendous amount of stress, and I didn't know how to deal with it. I hadn't learned the coping skills necessary to deal with grad

180

school and being an adult. Jules had never had to study at school, so she was unfamiliar with how much studying I had to do, or that I thought I had to do. I was redlining every single day because I didn't know how to wisely manage my time. When I got up each morning, it was like, "Ok, now I have to work until I go to sleep."

There wasn't much time to rest, and as I get older, I understand how valuable it is to be able to give your brain a break. You need time away from something in order for it not to consume you. I didn't know that at the time. Who knows, maybe I would have been a much better student if I had known how to block off my time to allow for more balance? I know that, as I have just turned 40, I can really tell the difference in the quality of my life when I block out time and be more balanced in my approach to work. It seems counterintuitive, but the more time I spend away from work now, the more productive I become.

Fighting in a relationship was very foreign to me. Unfortunately, it wasn't for Jules. She would see her parents fight a lot. I never saw my parents fight. Sure, my parents would get angry at each other, but they'd never yell and raise their voices at each other. That's something that started creeping its way into our relationship. The absolute bath of stress that I was in during law school didn't allow me to put the time into the relationship that I needed to in order to understand how valuable and important it is to be able to communicate with your partner. I know that now, but back then, I had no idea how important that would be. I feel that Jules and I have lost a great deal of time because we didn't know how to talk with each other. We kept focusing on how different the two of us were. We are, but that doesn't help the situation. It's when you can listen to the concerns of the other person and validate them that a relationship can really grow.

The fighting between us has dissipated with the better communicators that we have become. I think that most people don't have the patience for that. It's not a knock on them, but it's much easier to pull the ripcord on a relationship that may be struggling than to put in the work to understand what role each partner is bringing to the mess. With each passing year of being a lawyer, I feel as if I'm becoming a better partner. Being a better communicator has also helped me be able to deal with some exceedingly difficult people in my law practice, like Larry and the dude who threatened to kill me.

Mistrial a/k/a Legal Whoopsie

This is probably a good time for another flashback. Months before the trial, I had filed motions trying to exclude certain pieces of evidence from being brought up at the trial. In a trial, there are rules of evidence that are designed to keep pieces of information from being considered by the jury. You're probably familiar with this because you've seen "Law and Order" and heard someone say "objection!" But there are some things that you don't want to even be brought up at all during the trial. For instance, if the dude on trial for murder may have murdered someone before. If that gets brought up, even if it isn't true, it's game over.

For example, if a witness said that the guy on trial for drunk driving allegedly fucked a horse, there's no way that the people on the jury are going to forget that. Even if the judge said, "Ladies and Gentlemen of the jury, whether or not the defendant had sexual relations with a horse is not relevant to this case and you should disregard it." There's no way you're going to forget that. You're going to obsess over whether the defendant really did fuck that horse? How did he do it? Why did he do it? Was the horse good-looking? So that's why I filed motions to keep some evidence from even being talked about during trial. The prosecution agreed and they even stipulated to it. That means that they didn't have any problem with what I was asking for.

Specifically, I asked that there would be no mention of some of my client's past convictions, of which there were several. Like a lot. Like too many convictions. He was a repeat customer. A real consumer of criminal justice services. I also asked that there be no mention of allegations that my client tried to murder other people in the past. When I threw that request in there, I had no idea that it would become important because there's no way an allegation that my client had killed other people would be relevant evidence in this trial. There's no way that a prosecutor would ask that question during a trial, right? Ah, foreshadowing.

As soon as I figured out that I needed to object to this stupid question, I jumped up out of my chair. For some reason, the right side of my body got a head start on my left, and I ended up leaning to the left as I yelled "Objection!" Sidenote: It feels really good to say "objection" in court. I think being able to say it was one of the top 10 reasons that I became a lawyer. However, saying objection in court is what I'd think climbing the top of Mt. Everest would be like. Once you did it the first time, the thrill is gone.

I was fuming. Enraged. I was also scared. I'd never had something like this happen during a trial before. I asked myself, "Did I wait too long to object?" Instinctually, I relied on my training, and what I mean by that is what I've learned by watching lawyer television shows. I asked to approach the bench. My client turned to me in the clothes that I bought him and said, "What the fuck, bro?" Yes, what the fuck, bro, indeed.

The reason lawyers want to approach the bench isn't because the judge is old and can't hear, it's because you're going to say some shit that you don't want the jury to hear. As I started to walk toward the bench, I let the prosecutor go first. I saw his face, and he didn't look good. He looked pale, like someone had just run over his dog. I wanted to say to him, "dude, like what the fuck?" as my client so aptly summarized the situation, but I was in lawyer mode.

We both end up reaching the bench at the same time. It's an old hand-carved wooden bench. I don't know about wood, but it looked like maple. I could tell from the judge's expression that she could tell I was really pissed off. She didn't say anything, she just looked at me. I paused and took a deep breath to try and gather myself. Even though I was ready to go full beast mode up in here like DMX would have wanted, I let out a sarcastic laugh and matched it with a wry smile. The judge pushed a small black button, and it turned on some white noise so the jury couldn't hear what we were talking about. If I were a juror, that seems condescending and rude because I'd feel like a child. "Honey, cover your ears. Mom and Dad have to have an adult conversation. The white noise isn't something that's very calming to me. It just made me even more pissed off.

I delivered "Judge, we had an order covering this line of questioning! There's no way the answer to that question is relevant" in a very stern tone. I was surprised that I was able to come up with a coherent thought because all I wanted to do was yell "WHAT THE FUCK?!"

The judge nodded her head, acknowledging what I said, and turned to the prosecutor for his comments. His face now matched his white shirt, and he was even more pale. He didn't look good at all. If I were a betting man, his ass sweat percentage was in the high 90s. I don't think he was able to get out anything important. I could tell he knew he fucked up.

The judge turned to me again and asked, "What do you want to do?" I toyed with the notion of asking whether I could punch the prosecutor in the gut, but I didn't. I honestly didn't know what to do, but I wanted to make sure that I did the right thing. At the moment, I felt stupid because I felt like I should know what I wanted there and then. Looking back, I want to tell that kid not to put so much pressure on yourself. You didn't do anything wrong.

The best thing to do was to talk with my client about this colossal fuck up and find out what he'd like to do. I asked the judge for a recess so I could talk with my client. The judge agreed.

The prosecutor and I walked back to our respective tables. I felt relieved. Partly because I didn't absolutely lose my shit in court in front of the jury, and partly because I was cool under pressure and had the courage to stand up and say something. From experience, I can tell you that I've seen other lawyers just go along with things because they don't want to cause a problem. Even though letting something go may hurt their client. I felt pleased with myself, but in my last two steps around the desk, I knew that now was the time to do some real lawyering to figure out what to do. Basically, if I wasn't already, now I was going to be earning every last penny of that 60 bucks an hour.

The judge explained to the jury in a very high tone that we needed to take a break. It was kind of like a mom talking to the kids - "Mom's not mad at you. Sometimes adults have disagreements. We need to take some time and discuss it. Please go to your room and we'll tell you when you can come out." We waited in silence for the jury to be escorted from the room. They looked confused. I was pretty confused too. I didn't know what we were going to be able to do to fix it. Looking back, I was arrogant to assume that there was something I could do to fix it.

The door of the courtroom closed, and everyone left in the courtroom went about their way without saying a word. A deputy set me and my client up in a conference room to talk. As I sat down, I let out a really deep breath. It's weird how your body can trick your mind into thinking that it's physically tired when all you've been doing is sitting and standing up for a day. I let out a breath like I'd been breaking rocks next to Fred Flintstone over at the quarry.

I explained to my client what had happened. It was actually helpful that he had been through the criminal justice system before because he was familiar with relevance and objections. I

186

appreciated that he had let me do my job up until this point, even though he was familiar, because there are some idiots who think they're a legal expert because they did a Google search while taking a dump before court.

I explained that there were basically two routes we could take. First, we could ask for a curative instruction from the judge to the jury. That's something the judge would say, like, "Don't pay attention to what was said about the defendant murdering other people." The problem with that, like my horse fucker example before, is that people are going to think about it. To top it off, you just had the judge mention it again. So if they were sleeping earlier and missed it, chances are they're going to hear it now. I didn't think that was the best route to go, and I explained this to my client.

Second, we could ask for a mistrial. A mistrial is a do-over. It's saying this cake of justice that we have been working on was just dropped on the floor, and we don't think that we can fix it, so we need to start again. By "start again," it would mean that it would start again in a few months. I wanted to have to start this trial over again in a few months as much as I wanted a big old floppy dildo to spontaneously sprout in the middle of my forehead. However, at least with the dildo, I wouldn't have the buildup of anxiety for months until it came. No, that wasn't a pun. As I sat with my client in this room, I fidgeted and felt defeated. I put everything I had into every moment to get to this point in time. Now there's a good chance that I'd have to do it all over again.

It's funny how we treat jurors. We treat them like children. We think that because they aren't trained in the law that they are like children in the courtroom. What could have happened is that the judge, prosecutor, and I could have had a real conversation with the people on the jury and discussed what happened. The prosecutor could have had a heart-to-heart with them and said, "I made a mistake." It would have been a moment of humanity in the courtroom. Those, unfortunately, don't happen often. The robes

187

and the flags and the hardwood build up a sense of authority. If you fuck with whatever is going on in here, that person in the black robe is going to send you to jail. Courts deal with ideals and lofty notions; they don't deal with real humanity. They can't. At its overly simplistic level, it's just a man or a woman in a robe that we have trusted to make decisions for us when we aren't able to. For the people who participate in this system, saying that you were wrong is like saying you weren't worthy of the trust that was placed in you.

I knew what I had to do, but I didn't like it. I had to set aside my own self-interest and focus on my client's needs. It would have been much easier for me to just get this over with. What chance did I have to win anyway? This case was a stone-cold loser, and I was the one with the winning raffle ticket for a trip on a ship that everyone knew was going to sink. I'm sure I was capable of just saying "let's keep going" to my client, but there was a part of me inside that knew that wasn't what was best for him or what was best for the whole system in general. While I really wanted to keep going, I couldn't. What hurt the most was that I felt like I was making a difference, and now it wasn't even going to count. It's not even a win or a loss or even a tie; it's like it never existed.

It wasn't easy talking to my client. While there were times that he acted like he fully understood what was happening in the courtroom, this was a time that he didn't. He started arguing with me. I, the only person who was fighting for his dumb ass. He was yelling at me because he was like a caged animal who was going to have to wait several months before he knew what was going to happen. I understood why he was angry, but I didn't have the capacity to deal with his bullshit. I reverted from my lawyerly parlance to Nick, the pissed off human being. I couldn't keep up the facade any longer. I leveled with him like one man to another. I told him that what happened was fucked up, that it wasn't anyone's fault, but that he should ask for a mistrial because with the system the way that it is I don't trust that the jurors would ignore what they heard. He calmed down. By expressing to him that I was also angry and disappointed about what happened, I showed him that I cared, which I did. I learned a skill at that moment. I upgraded to another level of being a lawyer. There wasn't any cheery video game music, but I felt like I unlocked a new level of being a lawyer and human.

The judge instructed us to come back out into the courtroom to talk about what we were going to do. I was exhausted and reeling from what had just happened. I don't remember what I said. She let us know that she wanted us to write a brief on the legal issues presented by this afternoon's shit show. She wanted us to forward them to her and each other later this afternoon, and we were to come back to court at 9 am the next morning.

When I left the Courthouse that afternoon, I felt two inches shorter than I did when I entered it hours before. I felt beaten down. I didn't know what downtrodden meant before that day, but now I understand what that word means. In spite of that, I still had my chat with the deputies as I left the building. They're the ones that usually keep the judges and lawyers in check with their humor. I still smiled and joked around, but I'm sure they could see through the thinly veiled facade I was maintaining. I was angry. I wanted to fucking scream "THIS IS BULLSHIT!" and they probably would have agreed with me.

I made the long walk across the parking lot to my car, crossing the parking lines and looking around as I walked. I had held everything in long enough. I unlocked my Nissan Altima and threw my bag into the car so hard, it hit the passenger seat window. I sat down angrily, yes, you can sit down angry, and slammed the door. I started talking to myself. I asked myself the questions that I wasn't able to ask in court, or else I would go to jail. How the fuck could this happen? Why would you think you could ask a witness about other unproven allegations of murder of the defendant? God dammit, god dammit, god dammit! What the fuck, man? Now I gotta do this whole fucking thing over again!

It wasn't like I could relax; I had to go back to the office and do more work. More work because someone fucked this whole thing up. I drove faster than normal back to my office. Not even the lyrical skill of DMX could calm me down. I walked in through the back door of my office with even more anger than when I left the courthouse 25 minutes ago. I changed my clothes into my regular human clothes. I didn't untie my tie. I just threw it on the ground. It looked like a noose. Very poetic. Pulled the file out of my leather (I think it's leather) bag and spread it out on my desk. I sat there for a minute staring at it, not moving. I yelled "FUCK!" at the top of my lungs. Then I got to work. I'd never had to research the issue of a mistrial because nothing this fucked up has ever happened to me at trial.

I was familiar with the general concept of a mistrial, but needed some cases to support my point that this trial was FUBAR (fucked up beyond all recognition). However, searches for mistrial AND FUBAR yielded exactly zero results. In my elegant prose directed to the judge, I argued that the question asked by the prosecutor and answered by the liar on the stand was a bell, and that bell could not be unrung. I wanted to use the analogy that the moment after I lost my virginity, I couldn't be unfucked, but I don't believe it would have been well received.

I rushed to finish my research and writing. I spell checked everything and got it finished a couple of minutes before the 5 pm deadline that the judge gave us. Sending that email gave me the first sense of relief for the day. I was glad the day was over. I just sat in my office chair and stared at the wall for the next 14 minutes because I wanted time to myself. For those 14 minutes, I didn't have to stand up, sit down, or get something for someone. It was my time, and I wanted to spend it doing absolutely nothing.

After my 14 minutes of freedom, I realized there was a 93% chance that my calendar for the next 2 weeks just became open as fuck. I could have told people that, but I doubled down on my efforts to reclaim my time and started playing video games.

There's nothing like the freedom of playing video games in my law office. The juxtaposition of doing what some people consider to be a childish activity in an office where high-level adult shit takes place pleases me. It makes me feel happy, and I grin when I think of it. There are times when someone doesn't knock on the door to my office and comes in, and they see me playing video games, and I feel a pang of shame, but I'm not sure why. It does kind of feel like a mom coming into her 15-year-old son's room to do laundry, and she catches him jerking off, one of those kinds of moments.

That afternoon, before I went home, I played Football Manager. The name doesn't sound fun, but it is. It's a game about soccer, not American football. You don't even get to play soccer at all. You are the manager of a team, and you make all of the business decisions associated with running a team, like signing players, choosing formations and tactics, and figuring out player salaries. As I write this, it sounds like I'm actually trading time at one job for time at a virtual job, but I don't care. I love my team. No one is telling me what to do while I'm calling the shots, managing Sunderland Football Club.

I went home exhausted from a full day of court and the stresses of managing a digital soccer team. I didn't want to talk about what happened. I wanted to continue to retreat inward and ignore the situation. My wife, who loves to talk about everything, wanted to talk about it. I don't like talking about work at home. Home to me is a sacred place where shitty people and shitty things don't need to be discussed. Is that a sustainable way to live a life? Probably not, but I need sanctuaries. My wife, who's a psychic medium, told me I'm that way because I'm a cancer. That's a weird name for an astrological sign because you need to prep the person before telling them they're a cancer. Hearing that out of the blue can really hurt your feelings. "I'm a cancer? Well, you're an asshole! Oh, you meant the sign? Tee-hee-hee. I love you."

I told my wife about what happened, and her response tracked for a couple that's been together for as long as we have. "He threatened to kill you? What did you say to him?" My wife took the murderer's side.

I did feel relieved to go home and get a good night's sleep. Before I hit the hay, I checked my email incessantly, as I often do in the evening. Is it because I want to respond to email at night? Fuck no. After years of therapy, I've discovered it's because I'm looking for something to get angry at. If this person emailed me at 10:30 pm, I can call them an asshole, and it'll give me some relief when there's no reason I should have been checking my work email at 10:30 pm in the first place. That feeling of anger allows me to release a bit of steam that's been building up throughout the day. I can deal with things directly, but where's the fun in that? Telling someone exactly what you think is terrifying to me. What if they don't like me?

By now, you've probably discovered a huge thread in the quilt that's my personality. It's that I don't deal with things directly. I'd rather send a text than pick up the phone. I'd rather send an email than send a text. And for the love of God, I'd rather not deal with other people at all. Is that strange for a lawyer? A profession that entirely involves "other people"? Yeah, it's pretty weird. Well, I'm an interesting fig. There are a lot of layers to me. I'm not a seven-layer dip; I'm more like a twelve-layer dip. If you disagree, make sure you text before you call me.

After I vented about an email that a client sent to me at 10:47 pm, I headed off to bed, stammering and muttering under my breath like a crazy man you'd find wearing no shoes by the bus stop. I woke up early the next morning and made my oatmeal. It's a pretty boring breakfast as breakfasts go, but it's consistent and easy to make. As I ate my sad breakfast, I checked my email again. I was surprised that there was nothing from the prosecutor. That's pretty ballsy, considering the absolute fuck up that happened yesterday. The judge told us to get her a brief by 5 pm. "Ooh, you're gonna be in trouble" was the thought that kept playing on repeat. In my years of practice, I've discovered that prosecutors rarely have their feet held to the fire. It's like their Beau and Luke Duke down in Hazzard County. They can fuck up all they want, and no matter how bad it is, all returns to normal again in under half an hour.

I got to the office about an hour and a half before court and responded to emails. The nervousness began to creep into my asshole because I had to go to court this morning. Everything about court is the antithesis of who I am. The people, the anxiety, the pants. All of it. I'm baffled why I would choose a profession that would require me to go to court. It sounds weird, I know. Like a prostitute that hates sex. I got ready to leave and checked my email a few other times, and still nothing from the prosecutor.

The drive to court was unremarkable, and by that I mean I worried the entire way like I always do. I'm not sure what I think is going to happen when I go to court. At that point, I had been going to court for 10 years, and I had died. Not even once. No one broke my legs. There was no threat to my safety at court. I made it out of the shit each time, but my brain wanted to keep telling me that I was in danger. Other lawyers that I've talked to say that they don't get nervous going to court. Fuck them. I'm not sure if it's just bravado, because lawyers have a knack for exaggerating things, or whether they don't get nervous going to court. Someone told me that getting anxious about something means that you care about it. I don't think that's true, because I don't give a shit about court.

That Time I Thought
I Could Make a Difference

When I turned 35, I started getting restless being an attorney. I had been pursuing comedy for about two and a half years at that time, and I was feeling like I was stuck between the worlds of comedy and being a criminal defense lawyer. It wasn't a comfortable place to be in. I was staying up late and driving to shows and then getting up early and having to go to court and wait around for hours for 5-minute hearings when I could have just stayed in bed.

Then something happened. The judge who had been in St. Johns for multiple years decided that he was going to retire. He was a wild dude. There were always rumors floating around that he had two drunk drivings and wore a tether at times that he was on the bench or that his daughter was killed in a drunk driving, but I was never able to confirm any of that, so I don't think it's true. He was the second judge that I ever appeared in front of, and he was a trip.

When I was working at my first job being a lawyer, the attorney that I worked for was a real pile of garbage. I'm sure you're thinking, "Really, Nick, you weren't attracting the best people into your life? I'm shocked?" Yeah, me too, pal. Anyway, this attorney wasn't very well respected as a lawyer, and he was a real shitty mentor. He sends me up to handle a sentencing in a drunk driving case at the last minute. He says that he let the client know and that she was fine with it. Just get there early and talk, and then do the 5-minute sentencing. It'll be easy. I must have looked like a real rube back then.

I look at the file, and there's like nothing in there at all. I don't really have much of an idea what happened other than some chicken scratch notes on a yellow sheet of legal pad paper. I had no idea what was going to happen, and there's no way I was going to be ready for what would.

I get there early and find the court. I walk up to the counter, check in at the window, and see that my client for the morning has checked in. She's the only person who looks petrified, so I assume that it's her. I introduce myself and say that I'm going to be helping her with her sentencing hearing this morning. She looks at me like I'm nuts. Obviously, my "mentor" didn't tell her that I was going to be filling in.

I've been in this position a lot, and I can tell you that there are certain things in life that you're okay if someone unexpectedly fills in for someone else. Like you're driving someone to the airport or cleaning your house. However, people don't react well when you tell them that you're unexpectedly going to be filling in for their lawyer and the two of you have never met. It's never a good scene.

I knew it wasn't going to go well when I told this lady that, and her response was, "Oh my God!" like we were in a plane together and the captain just announced that we're going down. My eyes widened. This wasn't going to be a piece of cake like it had been described to me. This was going to be a footlong shit sandwich on pumpernickel.

The anxiety that she had was so strong, it probably set off the metal detectors downstairs. She puts her hands on her face and says, "I'm going to jail, I'm going to jail." Well, not if I can help it, lady, I thought. Jesus, calm down so I can help you.

I take a look at the presentence file and find out what happened. It was a typical drunk driving arrest. She was pulled over for speeding. There wasn't any bad driving. She had just been drinking and was unlucky and got pulled over and arrested. I didn't ask, but I guessed that wasn't how she wanted to spend her Friday night.

There's no way that I should be doing this sentencing with this lady freaking out, but I did. I wanted to call my boss and tell him he's a fucking terrible lawyer and he should have prepped me for this lady. I guess I needed to figure this out on my own. This was my journey, or whatever bullshit they say when times get tough in life. Why is my journey so goddamn difficult?

I talk with the lady and I tell her not to worry. I'm going to talk first, and then the judge is going to give her an opportunity to say something. I tell her that she is going to have to tell the judge that she is sorry for what she did, and that she has learned a lesson. There's no way she's going to do anything like this again. It'll be easy, I said.

We go into the courtroom, and I check in with the clerk. Now I've been in that courtroom for hundreds of hours, but in that moment, it was the first time that I had been there. They looked at me like and they knew I was an outsider. I looked like a big ol' piece of chum in the water wearing a khaki suit - don't judge me, it was the mid-2000s.

The judge comes in and the bailiff says, "All rise, the 65A District Court is now in session, the Honorable Richard D. Wells presiding," and we all sit down. Then I wait. And I wait. Then I have to take a piss, but I don't want to miss it when the judge calls my case, so I wait.

Just as my body tells me, "Hey dude, it's go time on this piss," the judge calls my case. I stand up, turn around and open the tiny quarter door that keeps the lawyers away from the riff raff people in the gallery. A classy move on my part, I thought. Oh, look at me, I'm wearing a suit AND I'm a gentleman. I'm crushing this lawyer thing already.

My client and I stand at the podium, and the judge says that we're here for a sentencing after my client pleaded guilty to Impaired Driving. The judge looks at me and says, "You're not Mr. Goldstein." I laughed and said, "I am not." The judge asks me, "How's Scott doing?" I hadn't been sworn in, so I was under no obligation to tell the truth. I wanted to say - as soon as I find that tiny Jew, I will be beating him with a rubber hose for the shit he pulled this morning. But I decided to go with "he's great, your honor."

Then he asks me whether my client and I had a chance to take a look at the presentence file. I said that we had and that we had nothing to add, correct, or delete. What normally happens next is the judge asks the lawyer to do what is called allocution. That's basically where you're arguing for your client. "He's a great guy, your honor." That's basically the strongest argument you can make. He's a really great guy, and they fucked up and they won't do it again." It's basically like you're apologizing for them, like if your kid stole a cookie from the cupboard. "Your Honor, Billy is a good kid. A real good egg. He didn't mean it, and he's awfully sorry."

But as I learned at that moment, this judge asks the defendant to talk first, not the lawyer. Again, something that my boss should have probably pointed out to the lawyer who had never been in that court and who was going to be defending the freedom of the most anxious lady in the tri-county area. The judge says, "Ma'am, what would you like me to know," and my client makes an audible noise and goes into total freak-out mode. She's breathing all weird, and it looks like she's going to cry. I'm looking around, and there are no tissues. Every criminal courtroom should have tissues. Sure, my client needed them now, but by the end of this hearing, I was probably going to need a few myself.

She says, "Nothing, your honor." Nothing, bitch?! I just prepped you for 20 minutes with a fantastic list of things to say, you wrote them down, and they're right there in front of your dumb face. Just say what is on the list. I reached over and tapped it with my left index finger and was like "remember this" with my face. I guess she was too freaked out, and she didn't want to say anything now.

Then the judge says, "Yesterday afternoon, I had some time, so I went outside here in downtown St. Johns." Ok, cool, that's nice, Judge. By the way, this dude was super old, but he was in fantastic shape. He was like one of those old soap opera stars that you'd find out were a hundred years old, and they looked amazing. He was always tanned, but he wasn't a dude who would tan, and the most striking thing was that he had this full, thick head of white hair. He kind of looked like Superman's dad. It was pretty intimidating.

Then he says, "I walked around and started asking people, would you be willing to die so (my client's name) could drive drunk?" I'm like, what the hell is this? Then he says, "They looked at me like I was a nitwit." I hadn't heard nitwit outside of a Looney Tunes cartoon before. Then my client decides to talk. She interrupts and says, "I'm sorry." I don't think the judge liked my client very much because instead of letting her off the hook, he followed up with, "Well, you will be sorry if you drive around drunk again and kill someone." A sob came from my client's face. Damn, this isn't the way I thought this morning was going to turn out, and I'm definitely not going to cover another hearing for another attorney ever again. I did, but that's at least what I said to myself at that moment.

The Ruling

I arrived at court and pulled into my usual parking spot, even though there was a red Chevy Cruze right next to it. I exited the Altima and put my suit coat on. I examined the parking lot. It was the same as yesterday. It was the same as the hundreds of other times that I'd arrived at the courthouse. I guarantee you it's the same at this very moment. I gathered my briefcase and walked inside. No small talk today. I wanted to learn what the fuck was going to happen. I stepped into the elevator and it moved up and down, like I was boarding a ship. I used my index finger to push the button for the fourth floor, and I stepped back and leaned against the back of the elevator. I checked my email again on the quick voyage. Finally, there was an email from the prosecutor. It had their response to the bullshit that happened yesterday. I was equal parts pissed off and anxious. Ass sweat protocol initiated.

The elevator dinged as it landed on the 4th floor. I was reading their brief as I stepped off. I knew the route from the elevator to the courtroom so well that I didn't have to look up. This response really was brief, "ay oh!". You'd think you'd put a little effort into trying to salvage the garbage fire you created that also happened to be a murder trial, but I guess that's just me. I pulled the first door and then the next to walk into the courtroom. It was stuffy inside.

The air was thick, like someone had farted in it a few hours earlier. As I walked in, I think someone said something to me, but I was too deep in thought to respond. It was hard to concentrate on what the fuck they were trying to argue because I was so pissed off. Sending the response to me minutes before court was a real bullshit move. I did my job and did what I was told. Because of that, they were able to read my response, review all of the cases I cited, and then formulate a response. I didn't have that luxury. I was struggling to calm myself down. I'm an incredibly emotional person when it comes to fairness. Things should be fair and equal, and when they are not, I flip the fuck out. Maybe that's why I chose this profession in the first place, because I wanted to work towards fairness and equality. I'm not sure because all I want to do is get in the face of this prosecutor and tell him, "That was fucking bullshit, bud."

I scribbled down a response to the ridiculousness that they wrote on a fresh legal pad from my bag. You'd think that if someone made a colossal screw up like this, there would be a bit of humility. There wasn't. It was a typical lawyer response. It ignored the bad facts. One law school professor told me, "If you have bad facts, argue the law. If the law doesn't support your position, argue the facts. If neither the law nor the facts support your position, then yell the loudest." Their response attempted to argue that the trial should go on. Basically, it was saying, "Nothing to see here, folks." It was worthless and a waste of time to read. If I were giving it a Yelp review, it would be one star.

I used my anxious, alligator brain to play all of this out in court ahead of time. I made the argument that I wrote in my brief, which was filed on time by the way, that double jeopardy should apply because the mistrial occurred as a result of prosecutorial misconduct. This strategy put the prosecution in a very difficult position, because if they agreed with me, then the charges would have to be dismissed, and the defendant would be able to walk out of the Jail with a plastic bag of all his shit and call for a ride and fuck off forever. He couldn't be tried again, like in that Keanu Reeves movie. If they didn't want door number one, they'd have to accept the fact that they fucked up by asking that question that they knew they shouldn't have. The choices were either "I knew what I was doing and did it anyway," or "I was too stupid to know that I shouldn't have asked this question." They call that a "Hobson's Choice." Having to choose between two equally shitty options is not something I would want to be named after. Sorry, Mr. or Mrs. Hobson. Actually, it's an old saying, so let's be honest here, it was probably about an old white dude.

I was so engrossed with reviewing their response that I lost track of the time and my surroundings. Even though I have terrible anxiety, staying focused when I'm under pressure is a positive quality I have. I'm able to zone myself out and focus on one particular task while things are happening around me. When I was studying for the bar exam, I studied for 12 hours one day and took one bathroom break. Afterwards, I didn't even realize that my wife had brought me lunch, and I ate it while I studied. Sure, it may have been the Adderall that I took beforehand, but who knows, right? I was in a similar mode this morning, sans Adderall.

"All rise" is an important phrase when you're in court. As soon as I heard it, I snapped back to reality, like a dog that was licking its balls and heard its owner come home. I gathered up all of my papers like a madman and dropped them on the old wooden desk. I looked like a detective who was going to be told by his boss, "You're too close to this case, Johnson." I straightened my suit coat and made sure my tie looked decent. I tucked the small part of the double Windsor knot in between the 2nd and 3rd button of my shirt like I always do. I was ready for battle. I was ready for battle, but I forgot my client. I panicked because I hadn't talked with him since yesterday. I debated internally that he didn't need to do anything this morning except sit there and not kill anyone, allegedly, of course.

As I was preparing to speak, a beautiful thing happened. The judge really laid into the prosecutor about what happened yesterday. A real ass chewing. With each word she spoke, she put me more and more at ease. The gooey part inside of me that responds well to fairness and equality was filled by what she said. Ass sweat protocol disengaged. She was pissed and let the prosecution know that. She mentioned the order that both sides had agreed to was directly on point. It was meant to keep out the topic of the prosecutor's question that fucked up everything. She mentioned that she was concerned with other parts of the prosecutor's case as well. I think to add a bit of even-handedness, she also scolded me for not objecting to some other questions that the prosecutor asked some of their witnesses. I didn't take it personally. I knew I could have objected to some of their questions, but my trial philosophy was "if it's not going to hurt my case, then I'm not going to object to it." Why risk appearing to the jury that I want to keep things out? My opening statement to them was to pay attention. It wouldn't look good if I followed that up with an objection to every possible question the prosecutor asked.

The judge continued on for several minutes and then railed at the prosecution about not filing their response when she asked for it. Up until that point, I thought they had just decided to send it late to me. It turned out that they didn't even get it done until that morning. In the words of Jason Bateman's character in Dodgeball, "That's a bold strategy, Cotton, let's see if it plays out for them." It turns out it did not turn out well for them. After 10 minutes of as big a dressing down as I've seen this judge give to another lawyer, she declared a mistrial, and we were done. She said that we would need to schedule a trial date, but needed time to get another jury panel in.

I left the courtroom with as much of a victory as possible. I felt like I made a difference. All too often, the prosecution gets away with a ton of bullshit. Many judges are former prosecutors, so they tend to side with the prosecution. It was refreshing to see a prosecutor get their ass handed to them by a former prosecutor. Maybe they'd learn from it and become a better lawyer? Probably not, but hell, it's nice to dream, right?

Money

People think that because I'm a lawyer that I have always come from money. That's not true. The first time that I lived in a real house was after my great grandpa died. It's weird to think that I was looking forward to another person dying so that I could move into a real house. But my great grandpa was a real piece of shit. I remember finding a photo in a drawer in his house of him in a KKK outfit. The KKK is such a pussy-ass organization. If you're going to be a piece of shit, then you should just own it. Don't run around playing some racist cosplay. I also found in another drawer some WW2 records indicating that one of my relatives was in the SS. That one hurt. I really didn't want to find that out. I should probably stop looking in drawers for things.

When I became a lawyer, I first worked for a real piece of shit. On the surface, he seemed like a great guy. He had a wife and two children and had his own general practice law office with a few employees. He lived in an amazing house in Okemos and was a part of the country club. It was like he had the perfect life.

I interviewed for a law clerk job after I graduated and came back to Michigan. I was looking for a place to earn some money while I was studying for the bar exam.

No one fucking knew what Catholic University of America was back in Lansing. I totally understand that because I had no idea what Catholic University was before I went there.

I remember meeting him during that interview. He was basically asking me. Why do you want to work here? He understood that I was probably too overqualified for what he was offering. The truth was that I had put out hundreds of resumes to firms in Michigan and got ZERO responses. I was like, "What the fuck? I graduated cum laude from law school." Now, I don't remember exactly what that means, but it meant that I worked my ass off. I outworked kids who were smarter than me. My dad died during law school, and I took two weeks off, and I was back and still graduated on time. And I get no fucking responses from law firms? Fuck that bullshit. I had to take something, so that's why I was where I was then.

I started working there for twelve dollars an hour. I had no idea what I should have been earning, and I was taking anything I could. If I had some options other than working at a restaurant, then I would have been able to have some leverage in salary negotiations, but I had to take what was available to me.

I learned quickly that this wasn't the professional office that I was hoping for. People were the most unprofessional that I'd ever experienced, and I worked at a used car dealership in high school. One of the receptionists had a crush on my boss and would wear low-cut shirts and was basically falling out of her clothes every day. She would basically try and fuck my boss every day that I was working there. She'd constantly make sexual innuendos and go into his office and basically put her titties out for him. She wasn't particularly good at it. You know how some people just know how to flirt? Well, this girl had no idea how to do it, and it was super annoying.

She was also terrible at her job. I was just above her in rank at the office. I'd ask her to do things like mail something for me, and she's just forgotten to do it. She knew that my boss would never get rid of her because there was a whole mess of shit that they knew about each other that they wouldn't want other people to know, so it just perpetuated a giant ball of wrong in the office every time that I was there.

One of the cool things about my boss was that he would bring me to his country club with him to play golf. I hated golf, but it was cool to be able to see how the rich people lived. There were Bentleys and BMWs in the parking lot of Walnut Hills Country Club. I'd never been around anything like that. I felt like I was owed that because of all the bullshit that I had to put up with in the office. I was doing a lot of work and was doing it at 12 bucks an hour, so yeah, you can take me to your country club and let me eat and drink for free once a week, bro.

This whole time, I was studying for the bar exam. When I came back from Maryland to East Lansing, I was planning on taking the July bar exam. I had just graduated in May. I was working all day, a few times per week, and then I was studying for the bar exam the other days of the week all day. It was so stressful. I signed up for a bar prep class, and it was so terrible. The instructors were so bad at their job. They had to teach material, I get it, but this doesn't have to be miserable. Find a way to come up with a story to make all of this bullshit make sense.

As the bar exam got closer, I decided that I wasn't going to take it in July. I felt like a failure. I felt like I had to keep going. I had pushed through this even after my dad died. I had to do this for him. I felt that if I postponed it until February, then I was letting everyone down. The problem was that I was exhausted. I had pushed myself so hard the past three years that I had forgotten who I was. I was constantly on the move.

When I went to law school in D.C., we were living in Baltimore, Maryland. It doesn't seem like the two are that far away, but it's one of the worst commutes in the U.S. I had to do it basically every weekday for two years. I was wasting so much time in the car every day. When I'd get home, I had no time to just relax. I'd have to eat dinner and get to studying for the next day. It was an onslaught of reading. If you didn't keep up with it, you'd drown. When my dad died, I got so far behind. I had to go back to Michigan to be with my family. I wasn't even able to really grieve because I kept worrying about what was going on back in D.C. What was going to happen? Was I going to lose the semester?

Luckily, Catholic University was amazing. Even though I was required to be in class so many hours per semester in order to be able to move on, they let it all go because of what I was going through. One of my professors sent me flowers and an amazing card to my mom's house in Michigan. I had no idea how they got that address, but it was something that really meant a lot to me.

I was tired. I didn't have anything left in the tank. It was difficult to do, but I gave myself some space to take a break. I didn't want to fail the goddamn thing, and I wasn't in the right space mentally to get ready for the bar exam. Getting ready for the bar exam is a whole new animal. I had done three years of law school, but law school is different than getting ready for the bar exam. For the bar exam, you're learning just what you have to know to be able to pass the class. On the other hand, with law school, you're being taught what the professor wants to teach and what's going to be on their exam.

It was also different because I was learning state-specific things since I was going to law school in Washington, DC. In my classes, they'd teach us what could possibly be on the Maryland or Virginia bar exams. If you wanted to know what Michigan would be teaching, then you'd have to learn that on your own.

For things like criminal law, it wasn't too much of a big deal because shit like murder is illegal in all 50 states. When I was going to law school in DC, I had no idea that I would be going back to Michigan. I wanted to stay in DC. I loved the area. I loved Baltimore. It was so much fun and different that Michigan and way the fuck better than Florida. When Jules got into Peabody and I had to transfer to Catholic University, I had every intention of living there after law school. But then my dad got sick.

It was such a bad time in my life that I don't remember how it happened, but I remember that after I transferred to Catholic, my mom told me that my dad was sick. He had been having a real hard time with acid reflux, and so he was taking a bunch of Tums to deal with it. Being the stubborn and hard-headed Leydorf man that he was, he put up with it and didn't see a doctor immediately. Honestly, I probably would have done the same thing, too. Things like that come and go. You eat some bad chili, and you're getting a lot of acid back up. It's not a big deal.

Unfortunately, he finally went to the doctor and had a scan, and they told him that it was cancer. Esophageal cancer. My dad wasn't a drinker. I think I saw him drink maybe 12 beers total in my entire life. He was a heavy smoker, however.

My mom told me, and I had no idea what to do. My first reaction was I don't have time for this. I'm in law school. I don't have the energy to go through this now. Stress has a tendency to make me feel selfish. I'm not a selfish person, but all I was doing was thinking about how this would affect me. I think it's another symptom of how sick law school made me. I was in this pipeline of getting this done that I lost sight of what really mattered. I could always go to law school, but I only had one dad, and he had cancer.

I had no idea what I should do. Should I stop school altogether and come back and be with my family, or should I soldier on and keep going? My dad told me to keep going. Looking back, I think that was the wrong decision. I'm not blaming him at all. He didn't want the sympathy. He said that he was going to be alright and not to worry about him. I should have known better than that. I should have quit altogether and spent the time to get to know my dad rather than racking up 100s of thousands in student loan debt. Law school would always be there, but family would not.

I went home as much as I could after my dad got sick. It was a 10-hour drive from Michigan to Baltimore, so that was tough, and the money that I did have was borrowed with interest from my student loans, so I didn't think it was a good idea to splash the cash around flying home every weekend.

I'd never seen my dad like this before. He was always a funny guy. He could be aloof at times, but he always would have a joke or tell me "get away from me!" when I'd go to hug him. I think he had a thing about being touched, which wasn't good news for him, having a son who loved to get a hug from his dad.

I have a lot of regret about not quitting school altogether. Some people would say that he wouldn't have wanted that. Well, this is my life, not his. I am the one who gets to choose because I'm the one who has to live with the consequences.

I don't remember much about what was happening on a day-to-day basis back then. Law school consumed my entire life. I should have been more involved and active with knowing what was going on with my dad, but I wasn't. I do remember that there was a time when a friend of his gave him a drink that supposedly would reverse the growth of the cancer. It was some black liquid that you'd have to drink, and it would magically make it go away. I think I should have paid attention more when I saw my dad try that. He wasn't the type of person who would believe in some magic beans like that. Looking back, it was more of a bleak situation than I remember. I am angry that someone took advantage of my dad with some snake oil because he was always someone I looked up to. He would tell you exactly what he thought of you and didn't care whether or not it came across all tied up in a neat little bow. He wouldn't fly off the handle on you, but he'd tell you if he thought you didn't know what you were doing. I saw him in a teacher union meeting once, and you could tell that everyone respected what he had to say. It was like they waited for him to chime in on the situation to hear his take.

I think my dad unknowingly practiced radical honesty, which is something that I'm getting into the older I get. It's basically centered around being honest with people and not hiding your feelings. If you make up some bullshit response when someone asks you how that dress makes them look, then you're doing both of you a disservice. Sure, there will be times when someone won't like what you have to say, but they'll respect you for giving them your honest opinion on the situation. There were so many times that I remember someone asking my dad if he'd want to do something for them, and he would straight up say, "No." He wasn't a dick about it. He just knew that he didn't want to do that. It wasn't like he didn't help people either. He would go out of his way to help kids in his class who were struggling with problems at home. I learned about that after my dad died because he wasn't one to brag about helping people. I really miss him.

I think we would have really gotten to know each other as we got older. I certainly would have appreciated some help with learning how to fix things around the house. He was good with that kind of stuff. He didn't push me into learning how to do things like that when I was a kid, but now I have no idea how to do shit, or even if I do, I'll fuck it up.

I remember his funeral very well. I had gotten the call that he had died early one Saturday morning. Jules went home to visit her parents and went to see my dad in the hospital. She didn't have to do that, but I will forever be thankful to her that she did. She went and sang him a song. I can only imagine how beautiful it was. I wish I were there for that, but I was in Maryland studying for a career that would end up not fulfilling me. I'm angry at the law because it's stolen half of my life. It just keeps going, and it doesn't care. No one feels sorry for you when you tell them you're a lawyer and you don't like it. This is your life, and if you don't figure out what the fuck you want to do, you'll end up wasting a lot of it.

They called me early that Saturday morning, and my phone was off. I woke up to hearing the answering machine message from Jules saying, "Sweetie, can you pick up the phone?" She was saying it in an extra nice and cute way, so I knew that something was up. She told me, and I fell down on the floor of our bedroom and started sobbing. I was alone. I was hundreds of miles away, and I missed spending the last minutes with my dad. He was gone forever, and I was left trying to figure out what our relationship meant to me because we didn't have any closure.

Jules was so great that morning. She told me that she had already called me a cab and booked me a flight home. She told me exactly what to do. I sat up and packed a bag. I went downstairs, and there was a yellow cab waiting for me outside my apartment building. I probably looked like a wreck outside because I felt like a wreck inside. The taxi driver was a Middle Eastern gentleman whose name I do not recall. I opened the door and got in. He said, My friend, how are you?" I channeled my dad and told him honestly, "My dad died this morning." He honestly said back to me, "Oh shit, my friend, I'm sorry, man. God dammit." We didn't talk the rest of the way to the airport. But I could feel the support from him. I could feel that he would look up from the rear view mirror to see how I was doing. I quietly sobbed a few times as we headed to the terminal.

As we parked in front of the airport, I just sat there. I didn't want to get out. I just wanted to stay here and not have to deal with that. An airport security guy came up to the window of the cab and tapped on the window, and said, "Let's get moving." The taxi driver responded sharply, "his dad just died. Give him a fucking minute!" I smiled and thanked him, and I got out of the cab. I forgot to tip him. I'm sorry for that, by the way. If the driver reads this book, hit me up, and I'll take care of you. He called me Habibi. He was a good egg.

I went to the ticket counter and I gave them my name. They must have seen that this was a bereavement fare, so the lady was really nice to me. She said that they didn't have any seats remaining in coach for the flight back to Detroit. I was preparing to have to wait at this airport for a few hours until they could find a way to get me to Detroit. She said, "Oh no, we'll be putting you in first class." I think it only ended up costing me a hundred dollars to fly first class from Baltimore to Detroit.

I can tell you that flying first class was the best thing about my dad dying. I got to board the plane first. Normally, I sit in the back with the cargo, so I have to board the plane last. Being a bigger guy, it's always awkward because I have to dance around people who are still putting their bags away. Getting on the plane first felt really cool, like I was part of a special club. It was quiet, and I had a moment to sit down and stretch out my legs. No one was sitting in front of me because I was in row one. I think they must have told the flight attendants that I was flying home because of a death because a middle-aged female flight attendant who looked like a mom came up to me and said, "I'm sorry for your loss." She asked me what I wanted to drink, and I said a Diet Coke. She came back in a few seconds with a Diet Coke and a can of regular Coke, and two tiny bottles of rum. She didn't mess around. I laughed, and she said, "Let me know if you need anything else." Well, yeah, I'd really like it if you could bring my dad back to life or maybe get me a new dad. Is there one in the overhead compartment next to the blankets? Then a head pops out and says, "Hi Nick, I'm your new dad. I'm proud of you. Call your mother, you know how she worries." But that didn't happen. I decided I was going to take advantage of this. I'd never flown first class before. Thanks, Dad, I guess, for the last gift that you ever gave me.

Not going to lie, I got pretty fucked up on the flight back to Detroit. In the quick, one-hour and thirty-minute flight. I had three beers and two shots. In the words of Doc Holiday in Tombstone, "Wyatt, I am [was] rolling." When the captain announced that we were making our final descent into Detroit, I remember being like "No!" Can we just keep flying up here for a while? My dad isn't dead up here, and there's a nice lady who keeps bringing me drinks.

But I guess we didn't "have enough fuel" to fly around all day. Psht! Whatever. So we finally landed in Detroit. I was feeling pretty buzzed. As we landed, I remember audibly saying "whoow!, like a kid on a rollercoaster. I'm sure the flight attendant was thinking that it was perfect timing to get my ass off this plane because there wasn't enough booze on it to fill the dad-sized hole in my life.

Also, the irony of flying from Baltimore to Detroit wasn't lost on me. It was like flying from Mordor to a place a little better than Mordor. Honestly, both Detroit and Baltimore were absolute shit shows in the early 2000s. Crime was high. Baltimore had the highest number of murders in the country. They filmed the show "The Wire" a few blocks away from our apartment in Baltimore, which made me think about my life choices. Maybe we should have found a place in Virginia?

But I loved Baltimore. Charm City. I didn't find it that charming, really. But I liked it. It felt real and honest. There wasn't any bullshit about the place. You know, with some bigger cities, they have this kind of fog around them to make it seem like the place is better than it was? Baltimore didn't have that. The people were nice. Even though I was a white dude, I felt like everyone really accepted me. When I lived in Miami, it felt like everyone was segregated. In Baltimore, there was a lot of segregation, with certain neighborhoods being socio-economically organized, but everyone seemed to be nice to one another. I had no idea who was murdering whom in that city, because I never felt unsafe there. True, I didn't go a few blocks west of my apartment on Charles Street, but I felt like everything was okay and that I wouldn't get murdered if I did.

One funny Baltimore story. One early winter weekend morning, we got about half an inch of snow. Coming from Michigan, that wasn't a big deal for me. But everyone in the city was flipping the fuck out about it. I remember Jules and I went to the garage across the street to get my Mazda, yes, we traded in the Monte Carlo after Jules puked in it after a night of drinking with some of my work colleagues. We got to the Mazda, and the back driver's side window was smashed in. They had taken my CD collection. Wow, that makes me sound old. Only your grandpa has a CD collection in 2020. I was like, "Oh no, my Limp Bizkit CDs!" It was disappointing.

Remember that I'm super white, so I haven't been the victim of a crime before. I called 911 to report that someone had stolen my CDs from my car. In Baltimore. The murder capital of the United States. A nice lady picked up the phone and said, "911, what's your emergency?" I'm like, "Yeah, my car was broken into and they stole my CDs." This lady was a real professional because I could only detect slight laughter on her end. Knowing what I know now, if I were her, I would have told myself that I had to put myself on hold for a second and then told everyone in the call center, "We got a real idiot over here on Charles Street that had his car broken into, y'all! (pause for uproarious laughter). But, to her credit, she didn't.

What she did say was that the police weren't responding to non-emergency calls that morning. Umm, what? I'm a white man. How are you going to tell me that the police aren't going to respond to my 911 call? She explained that the police weren't responding that morning because of the snow emergency. What snow emergency? Is there some squall or whatever heading right toward us? No, you mean the dusting of snow on the ground? There wasn't enough to make a snow angel. She told me that I could come down to my local precinct and make a report if I wanted to. Umm, that's okay. If the police have too much trouble navigating through half an inch of snow, I don't think they're going to track down the guy who now has all of my amazing CDs. It's frustrating, too, because with all of the snow, there was probably a footprint or two.

I went downstairs to the man who was managing the garage that morning. I guess I disturbed him or something because he was asleep. I had to do the thing where you want to politely wake someone up, so I banged into something. From the sounds of it, it wasn't his first rodeo because the first thing he said, even before opening his eyes, was "how can I help you?" Sorry for waking you, sir, but my car was broken into. Do you have any security tapes I could look at and show to the police? Umm, yeah, no. What are those cameras for? Are they on? I don't think they've ever worked, he replied with little or no concern. Well, my car was broken into. He immediately responded, "You park your car here at your own risk." Wow, thanks. If this wasn't the only available parking garage that was affordable within walking distance from our apartment, I would have driven my Mazda hatchback with a broken-out rear driver's side window into his fucking office.

Now, back to my dead dad. We had just arrived in Detroit, and I was hammered and getting more drunk by the minute. A cool thing was that I was going to be able to get off the plane first. That's never happened to me before. Normally, I'm back with the cattle and freight in coach, where people don't give a fuck about how much time it takes them to get off the plane. "I'm going to take this moment to finally get rid of this hangnail while I stand in the middle of the aisle." Get the fuck outta my way, grandma! But I didn't have to toil with the idiots this time. I was able to disembark quickly. Again, I really just wanted to stay on the plane this time. I didn't want to have to deal with everything that had just happened. I was starting to feel numb, and it wasn't from the alcohol or the freezing cold weather here in Detroit, it was having to deal with the fact that I'd never see my dad again.

As per usual, I used humor to deflect real emotions. As I unbuckled my seat belt and stood up, I felt how drunk I was. I wasn't stumbling around or anything like that. I'm fairly good at handling my liquor, I mean, I went to a Big Ten school for undergrad. Drinking was basically a 2-credit class that met every weekend.

The flight attendant apparently had forgotten by this point that my dad was dead, and she said, "Have a great time in Detroit." I responded with a drunken "Can I get a few beers for the road?" They all laughed, but I was kinda serious. I had an hour and a half drive from Detroit back to Bannister, and this buzz wasn't going to last that long.

I walked off the plane and down the tube thing, like I was being delivered again into an existence where I only had one remaining parent. It was weird because I didn't know anyone whose parent had died, and I was born by cesarean.

I walked through the terminal, and down the hall was Jules. She was half smiling, half crying, and looking as beautiful as ever. We didn't say anything. I just navigated toward her and hugged her, and started sobbing. She pulls back and says, "Are you drunk?" Umm, yeah, I was flying first class for the first time, and my dad died, so I thought it would be a good time for an early morning drink. "I've had a few," I said with a wry smile. Then I suggested something about the Mile-High Club and an airport bathroom. It wasn't one of my finer moments, but who are you to judge me? Did your dad just die?

The car ride home was basically me sitting there getting sober by the minute, and Jules talking about what happened, and me not paying attention. Funny enough, that would describe most of our early twenties life together. I was having a hard time figuring out what exactly was happening, and the booze wasn't helping either.

After making it back home, my family was in full funeral preparation mode. They were talking about when and where, and who was going to be doing what. They were talking about who they would ask to say something at my dad's funeral. They were discussing different options. High school friends, college buddies, work folks. I interjected and said, "I'll do it. I want to say something." I guess I was still drunk. No one talked me out of it, so they put it in the bulletin for the funeral that I would be a speaker. I remember Jules saying, "Sweets, do you really want to do that?" I felt like I needed to. This was my dad. I didn't want anyone else to say something at his funeral if I didn't. Plus, it would be nice to get some great public speaking experience, right? There's no more pressure than having to speak at a funeral, let alone your dad's. My mom was absolutely devastated, but she did what my mom normally does and found a few short pieces for me to read while I was up there. I really appreciated that. I had no idea what I was going to say.

I recited a poem. I don't remember what it was. I made it through the first 17 or so words and then broke down into full-on sobbing. This was beginning to feel like it was a mistake to speak at my dad's funeral, but I made it through it. I made 'em laugh with a couple of stories about my dad and then fucked off into the afternoon, and for the next few hours I was remembering him. Then reality squeezed its way back in, and I was focusing on how I needed to get back to DC so I could finish school.

Earning Every Penny

Weeks passed following the mistrial. Many lawyers had heard about it and asked me what happened when I saw them in court. They congratulated me on the work that I did for my client. I didn't think too much of it at the time, but with each person that mentioned it, I felt like I actually did win. My time wasn't wasted. I learned something important about myself - when push came to shove, I wouldn't back down. I had doubts before that and, honestly, continue to have doubts about that to this day, but I can look back on the work I did in this case as evidence that I had a backbone. Even though I hated going to court, I could practice law at a high level. I earned every cent of that $60 per hour.

As more weeks flew by, negotiations started heating up. The prosecutor went from not wanting to talk about resolving the case to mentioning it every time I'd see him in court. My client, by holding firm and showing that he had the stones to see this thing all the way through, had cemented in the prosecutor's mind that he wasn't someone that could be fucked with. My client gave zero fucks. To me, my client was like Bane from the Christopher Nolan Dark Knight Batman movies. Alfred would call him the kind of guy who liked to watch the world burn, allegedly. Taking a position like that can turn out to be a genius move if the party on the other side has any doubts. They learned my client has no problems pushing all of his chips into the middle of the table (I'm sorry for the poker reference) and isn't concerned if the odds were not in his favor (yes, a Hunger Games reference).

The prosecutor didn't want to go to trial again. I found satisfaction in that because it showed my trial strategy worked. If at the first trial I demonstrated that I was a complete moron in the courtroom, then they'd have no problems starting the trial again after the mistrial, but that's not what happened. They came back to me with a plea offer of 20 years in prison with the possibility of parole. Honestly, I didn't think that was a fair offer considering the bullshit that I just went through. But this is one of the situations where you have to follow the rules of being a lawyer and not just being a normal human being, or "normie." I wanted to tell them to go fuck themselves, because I was still steaming like a bucket of clams after the shit show that was the first trial, but I had an ethical duty to communicate their plea offer to my client. That meant I had to go all the way out to the jail where they were keeping my guy in Charlotte, Michigan. He couldn't stay in the jail where the trial was being held because 4 of his best buds were also guests there. The jail didn't want to have a "why the fuck did you testify against me, bitch?" party in their jail, so they thought that it would be best if they kept them apart.

It was such a pain in the ass to have to go to Charlotte to see my client. What year is this, 1950? Can't I see him on Skype or some shit like that? Why did it take a pandemic for the criminal justice system to start using technology that we came up with in the year 2000? If you call a jail and ask if you can talk with a client, they put the phone down so they can have a hearty laugh. There's no way to just put the dude on the phone? I can guarantee he's not doing anything other than probably crocheting himself a scarf or angrily masturbating.

I got in the Altima and felt a sense of pride as I drove to Charlotte. They pronounce it Char-LOTTE, not CHAR-lotte. It's a weird place. Not my favorite place to go. Not my favorite jail to visit either. The Wi-Fi sucks there. I arrive at the jail, and I have to fill out a form. Then I do what I normally have to do when I go to see clients in a jail: I wait, like a long time. By in large, the people who work at jails don't give a shit about defense attorneys. We're looked at as second-class citizens. No one thinks of being nice to a criminal defense lawyer. That is, until you need one. Look, I'm not looking for a high five or a hand job, I'm just looking to have my time valued like every other human being. There are times that I have driven to go see clients, and I get to Charlotte 10 minutes before visiting hours end, and they won't let me see my client. For real, dawg? I just drove all the way out to your stupid town, and now I have to drive back and then drive back again to see my client? No wonder no one lives in this bumfuck place.

Shift in Mindset

As I was writing this book, I did the classic Nick Leydorf thing and set an unattainable goal of trying to get it done in a month. If that sounds crazy, that's because it is. It was a pretty fucking dumb idea. I thought I could do it, though. I set a goal of writing for at least 45 minutes a day in the morning. If I wrote 1500 words, I'd knock off early for the day. If I didn't, I'd just sit there while the cursor blinked on and off. If you try and have a staring contest with a cursor, the cursor always wins in a blowout.

Contrary to the Facebook ads that flood my feed, you can't write a good book in 30 days because you're going to burn yourself out. Unless you're these goddamn robots that are stealing our jobs. If a robot comes for my job, I'll fistfight it. Don't get me wrong, it's good to have goals. Normal ones. Not writing a good book in 30 days kind of goals. No one can attain that. I don't want to debate here. It's not one of those "shoot for the moon and if you miss you might hit a star" bullshit memes that your aunt posts on Instagram.

I feel like I'm close to unlocking a new chapter of my life. It's a shift in mindset. In my first 40 years, I was always anxious. I felt like I needed to be doing something at all times. If I wasn't moving, I was dying. Don't buy into that mindset because you're going to end up unhappy and anxious. Don't get me wrong, I'm still anxious. Something just feels different.

As I underwent the painful task of editing this book, I discovered one thing about myself in particular. Whether it was when the jerk threatened to kill me, or Larry, I have a persistent urge to be liked. If that feeling resonates with you, then do whatever you need to do to remove that parasite from your being now. Treat it like a tumor because it is one. Linking your self-worth with the approval of others has sapped so much of my time and energy. I've seen the endgame of that desire. I'm not going to be able to make everyone like me. It's impossible. Some shithead like Larry isn't going to like me. Even though he's wrong, I gave him that power and control over me.

Throughout my life, adversity and conflict would pop up, and I'd shit myself with fear because I thought that if someone didn't like me, I'd die. Well, once you embrace that not everyone is going to like you, then you'll be able to start living. I'm not a fucking yogi. I'm just a 40ish-year-old dude. I'm just navigating life every day like everyone else, but I've found when I stray way from the mantra "not everyone is going to like you, just embrace that," I become unhappy. It's like using a metal detector, I can't tell you exactly where and how to uncover it within you, but when you're on the right path, there's something that goes off and will tell you where you need to dig.

The other thing that I've taken too long to figure out is that it is profoundly important to just fucking relax. I need to feel more and not think so much about what I should be doing. Restlessness is the force that muddies the water that making me unable to see things clearly. I have a problem with sitting still. I have to be doing something at all times. If I am not moving, then I feel like I'm going to be left behind by the world.

I've always been chasing the next thing, never satisfied with where I am or what I've accomplished. But lately, I've been trying to just sit with my thoughts more. Being present. It's fucking hard, y'all. My mind wants to race ahead, plan the next move, worry about what's coming. But I'm realizing there's value in stillness. In just being.

The other day, I was sitting on my back porch, watching the trees sway in the breeze. Nature has just been for longer than any of us have existed and will be there well after we're all gone. For once, I didn't reach for my phone or try to fill the silence. My leg wasn't bouncing up and down. I just sat there, feeling the air on my skin, listening to the leaves rustle. Doing nothing. And you know what? It felt fucking amazing. Peaceful. Like I was exactly where I needed to be in that moment. Then I remembered a work email that I didn't send about a ridiculous fight between siblings over trash in a storage unit. Doing nothing ended, and the anxiety rushed back into me.

Don't get me wrong, I may always have that restless energy. That drive to achieve and push forward. But I'm learning to balance it with moments of calm.

I have a desire to achieve, to accomplish something, so I keep moving in order to do that. However, and listen up if you haven't been already. When you do something without knowing exactly what it is that you want to do, you're just wasting time. I think that sums up my becoming a lawyer - I knew that I wanted to do something that was extraordinary. I saw the law and being a lawyer as a way to achieve that, so I just started out on that path without taking a hard look at what it would look like when I got there. It turns out that I learned a bunch of helpful things along the way, but I didn't need to become a lawyer to do any of that. Had I just calmed myself down and looked inward to figure out exactly what my goals were in life, then maybe I could have allowed myself to take a different path. Maybe I would have been able to be more focused, maybe I would have started doing stand-up comedy 15 years earlier.

I've been in my head for most of my life. I don't want to get all fucking woo-woo here but I think this is important. There's what's in your head and what's in your guts. I have listened to my head way more than I've listened to my guts. For me, my head is the voice that says you should and have to do X. My gut is what I want to do. For me, being ruled by the shoulds and have-tos has led to a life of unhappiness. If I had listened to my guts, then I wouldn't have waited until I was 40 to figure this shit out. While I'm no Tony Robbins, I think I'm close to unlocking the meaning of life. I haven't pieced it all together yet, but it involves disregarding the opinions of others and a Chipotle burrito. Of course, with guac because you matter.

Communication Breakdown

This time, I plan it out perfectly so I will have enough time to discuss the prosecutor's new offer with my client. I see the nice lady behind the bulletproof glass, and I hand her my green form with my name, date of birth, and bar number on it. They want me to fill out my home address on it, but they can get bent. No one in this building needs to know where I lay my head at night.

She tells me to have a seat, and I do. I sit in the one chair in the middle of this room. The architecture is not impressive. Everything is brown and somehow there's carpet everywhere. There's even carpet on the walls. "Hey Gus, we have all this extra carpet. What should we do with it? GUS: Uhh, put it on the walls!" I can't imagine the weirdo who approved this color palette. Let's make the whole place look like diarrhea. I plop myself down into the kind of chair you'd see outside of a high school guidance counselor's office. I peruse the reading materials on this broke-ass desk next to me. There wasn't much to peruse. There was an ESPN magazine from 14 months ago and a Highlights magazine. I wasn't interested in reading about old news that I didn't give a shit about 14 months ago, and all of the games in the Highlights were already done. It made me sad to think that there were kids who were waiting to see their family members in jail. If I went to jail, I wouldn't want my kid to come see me there. I don't look good in yellow, and I never want my son to see my feet with Crocs with "Property of County Jail" on them. I decided to sit there and stare into space and complain to myself how stupid it was that I was the only person in this lobby, and I had to wait for an inmate. The nice lady interrupts my internal pity party and tells me that they're ready for me. "Yay!" I put a big old grin on my face and utter a smart-alecky "Thanks," as she buzzes me into the next door. I walk to the next steel door and smell the sadness of this visitation room. It buzzes, and I open the door and go inside.

I wait again for my client and see his tiny frame appear through the window as they buzz him in through the door on his side of the steel fence that separates us both. I tell him why I'm there to visit him, and I share the prosecutor's offer. I tell him that I think I can do better. I tell him that I think they don't want to have to take this case to trial again. As I waited for his answer, I assumed that I was dealing with a rational individual. I assumed that he would know what common sense was and what the possible outcomes were going to be because he sat in court next to me throughout the first trial. I don't know why I thought that my client would now be willing to listen to reason after the month had passed since the mistrial. I also didn't think he was going to tell me to go fuck myself, but he did.

Actually, he did more than that. I'm not talking about the whole threatening to kill me thing, because he totally did that. He started the chain of events inside of me that needed to happen. His aggro, "I'm gonna kill you, motherfucker," awakened the sensitive kid inside of me that needed to be true to himself. What I had been doing for all of those years wasn't a sustainable business model. If I kept on the same trajectory, I would have had an aneurysm while taking a shit or climbed a clock tower with a high-powered rifle. There are moments in your life when shitty things happen to you. Things that you didn't plan on. You can't reverse time and keep them from happening. Don't bury them inside of you. Use them to transform into the person that's inside of you waiting to come out. I knew for years that I didn't want to go to court and fight anymore, but I didn't know how to get unstuck. I didn't know what I wanted to do, but I knew that I didn't want to do that again. Even though at the time I was terrified, without this guy whom I will probably never see again, and I'm totally fine with that, I wouldn't have made the changes in my life that have brought me to the point where I am now. For that, I am grateful.

Epilogue

I'm not exactly sure what "epilogue" means, so I probably shouldn't be using it. I wanted to say something at the end, even though I fucking nailed it. I wanted to say that what that Greek guy said a long time ago about not being able to step into the same river twice is true.

I can't remember his name. I'm pretty sure it was Steve. Anyway, I am struck by the impossibility of ever truly experiencing the same moment twice. Even if I wanted to go back and relive my life and make different choices, who knows whether it would make any difference? Time is a raging current that drags us along, leaving only fragments of memory in its wake. We're always evolving. We're constantly changing. I've transformed countless times since I started this crazy project of writing a book. As my fingers type out my thoughts across the keyboard, I can't help but notice how different I am from when I first started writing this goddamn book. My hair was longer (relatively speaking), my posture straighter, and my outlook on life seemed headed in a much more positive direction. The editing process made me read and re-read passages, and I don't recognize the person I was when I wrote them. The words on the screen reflect my evolution, and I couldn't be prouder. My midwestern upbringing makes me feel cringy when I direct the word proud toward myself, but the work I've done here has made it a little more palatable.

As I take the time to look back on this monumental task of writing a book, it seems like my guts had a better sense of direction than my brain when it came to choosing the path to take in life. Maybe if I trusted my gut sooner, I wouldn't have spent so much time stuck in my head like a lost tourist following a glitchy GPS. It's like choosing between two travel companions - one is a reliable guide with a map, while the other is your gut feeling whispering, "Trust me, I know a shortcut... through this Chipotle." And hey, who knows, maybe that Chipotle burrito with guac, because you matter, does hold the secret to unlocking the mysteries of the universe!

If I kept waiting for the perfect version of this to flow from my head onto the page, I would have never put it out. For better or for worse, this is me. There are a lot of parts of me, and I bet there are a lot of parts of you, too. Be kind to them. Listen to those voices in your head. Within reason. If you're a mailman and the dogs are talking to you, then you may want to get someone to help with those thoughts, fam. Those voices are your guts. They know what the fuck they're talking about. Like Cosmo Kramer said, "You gotta listen to the little man! The little man knows all." All right. Good talk. I'll see you out there.

Acknowledgments

This book exists because of the generosity, time, and encouragement of friends who showed up when it counted. Robert Jenkins, Jacqui Marpa, Alexa Stanton, and Simon Carlson—thank you for your thoughtful reads, blunt edits, and steady belief. Your fingerprints are on every page, and I'm better for it.

www.ingramcontent.com/pod-product-compliance
Lightning Source LLC
Chambersburg PA
CBHW021233130626
46554CB00004B/1470